Sri Lanka

WORLD BIBLIOGRAPHICAL SERIES

General Editors:
Robert L. Collison (Editor-in-chief)
Sheila R. Herstein
Louis J. Reith
Hans H. Wellisch

VOLUMES IN THE SERIES

VOLUME 20

Sri Lanka

Vijaya Samaraweera
Compiler

CLIO PRESS

OXFORD, ENGLAND · SANTA BARBARA, CALIFORNIA
DENVER, COLORADO

British Library Cataloguing in Publication Data

Samaraweera, Vijaya
Sri Lanka. – (World bibliographical series; 20)
1. Sri Lanka – Bibliography
I. Title   II. Series
016.9549′3   Z3211

ISBN 0–903450–33–X

Clio Press Ltd.,
55 St. Thomas' Street,
Oxford OX1 1JG, England.

ABC-Clio Information Services,
Riviera Campus, 2040 Alameda Padre Serra,
Santa Barbara, Ca. 93103, USA.

Designed by Bernard Crossland
Typeset by Columns Design and Production Services, Reading, England
Printed and bound in Great Britain by
Billing and Sons Ltd., Worcester

THE WORLD BIBLIOGRAPHICAL SERIES

This series will eventually cover every country in the world, each in a separate volume comprising annotated entries on works dealing with its history, geography, economy and politics: and with its people, their culture, customs, religion and social organization. Attention will also be paid to current living conditions – housing, education, newspapers, clothing, etc. – that are all too often ignored in standard bibliographies; and to those particular aspects relevant to individual countries. Each volume seeks to achieve, by use of careful selectivity and critical assessment of the literature, an expression of the country and an appreciation of its nature and national aspirations, to guide the reader towards an understanding of its importance. The keynote of the series is to provide, in a uniform format, an interpretation of each country that will express its culture, its place in the world, and the qualities and background that make it unique.

SERIES EDITORS

Robert L. Collison (Editor-in-chief) is Professor Emeritus, Library and Information Studies, University of California, Los Angeles, and is currently the President of the Society of Indexers. Following the war, he served as Reference Librarian for the City of Westminster and later became Librarian to the BBC. During his fifty years as a professional librarian in England and the USA, he has written more than twenty works on bibliography, librarianship, indexing and related subjects.

Sheila R. Herstein is Reference Librarian and Library Instruction Coordinator at the City College of the City University of New York. She has extensive bibliographic experience and has described her innovations in the field of bibliographic instruction in 'Team teaching and bibliographic instruction', *The Bookmark*, Autumn 1979. In addition, Doctor Herstein coauthored a basic annotated bibliography in history for Funk & Wagnalls *New encyclopedia*, and for several years reviewed books for *Library Journal*.

Louis J. Reith is librarian with the Franciscan Institute, St. Bonaventure University, New York. He received his PhD from Stanford University, California, and later studied at Eberhard-Karls-Universität, Tübingen. In addition to his activities as a librarian, Dr. Reith is a specialist on 16th-century German history and the Reformation and has published many articles and papers in both German and English. He was also editor of the *American Society for Reformation Research Newsletter*.

Hans H. Wellisch is a Professor at the College of Library and Information Services, University of Maryland, and a member of the American Society of Indexers and the International Federation for Documentation. He is the author of numerous articles and several books on indexing and abstracting, and has also published *Indexing and abstracting: an international bibliography*. He also contributes frequently to *Journal of the American Society for Information Science, Library Quarterly*, and *The Indexer*.

To my Mother and Father

Contents

Contents

Contents

Introduction

Sri Lanka, the 'Resplendent Isle', is the smallest of the South Asian states. Sri Lanka was not the name by which the island was always known. The Greeks knew it as Taprobane, the Arab seafarers as Serendib, the early Europeans in Asia as Zeilan or Seilan, and the British as Ceylon, the official name which was retained until 1972 when the country was renamed Sri Lanka. (Consistent with contemporary scholarship, I shall use the name Sri Lanka in the annotations even when discussing materials which refer to the country as Ceylon). Whatever name was used, from Ptolemy's time onwards the island was readily identifiable on a map, tear-shaped and suspended at the tip of the subcontinent of India.

Sri Lanka is a compact island: in extent 25,332 square miles, it is only 270 miles long and 140 wide. It is separated from the subcontinent by a strip of sea, not more than 22 miles wide in some places. It has a strikingly varied topography: sandy beaches fringe its coastline, plains dot its northern, eastern and southern parts, and a series of plateaus meet the plains and extend to a central mountain mass with craggy peaks, the highest of which stands at 8,282 feet. The island's climatic year is dominated by two monsoon seasons – the main south-west monsoon (late May to late September) and the secondary north-east monsoon (December to February) – and rainfall functions as the principal parameter of seasonal changes. Rainfall is also the key factor in the demarcation of the island into two geographical regions, the 'wet zone' and the 'dry zone' – the wet zone, the south-west quadrant, receives heavy, well-distributed and reliable rainfall and the dry zone, which covers by far the greater land mass, receives less reliable and restricted rainfall.

Sri Lanka's geographical location has been of crucial importance from prehistoric times. The island's proximity to India has been an inescapable factor in the making of its peoples and their

xiii

civilizations: Sri Lanka's principal communities originated from the subcontinent as did its major religions, and throughout its history, institutions, ideas and beliefs have flowed freely from the subcontinent into the island. However, the insularity of Sri Lanka has ensured that its peoples would evolve differently and that their civilizations would not simply replicate things Indian – indeed, while Indian influences are traceable, its peoples have moulded their culture and society into something unique and distinctive. Sri Lanka's central location in the Indian Ocean made it a focal point of seafaring trade, exposing it to currents of influences from both the East and West. The island was known to the Mediterranean World – Ptolemy offered a brief but vivid description of Sri Lanka in his *Geographia* – and with its increasing importance in the spice trade beginning in the 15th century, it was to be brought within the orbit of interest of the European trading powers.

Sri Lanka's population (nearly 15 million at the 1981 census) is conventionally divided along two lines: ethnicity and religion. Race, culture and language are the factors determining ethnic identity. There are two principal ethnic groups, the Sinhalese (comprising 74 per cent of the population) and the Tamils (12.6 per cent), and a host of smaller ethnic groups – most notably, the Muslims (7.1 per cent), Indian Tamils (5.5. per cent) and Burghers (0.3 per cent). Religious differences have produced four principal groups: Buddhists (69.3 per cent), Hindus (15.5 per cent), Christians (7.5 per cent) and Muslims (7.5 per cent). Religion cuts across ethnic boundaries, with the result that social groups, united at one level by commonly perceived ethnic identity, are differentiated at another level on the basis of religious beliefs. Beyond the conventional demarcations lie other factors which have created different sets of boundaries, among which regional differences and caste are the more significant. The result is a complex ordering of society, one which has made the understanding of the relations among the constituent social groups a far from easy task.

The presence of both the Sinhalese and Tamils goes back to the very beginning of Sri Lanka's history, although it is unclear exactly when the respective communities first settled in the island. Tradition traces the first Sinhalese settlement back to the 5th century BC when Prince Vijaya, their legendary founding father, arrived from North India. Vijaya and his followers colonized the dry zone region that came to be known as the *rajarata* (king's country), and it was here that their descendants produced flourishing civilizations centred on two kingdoms, Anuradhapura (3rd century BC to 995) and Polonnaruva (1017 to 1215). There is controversy as to whether the island was already populated by Tamils from South India by the time of Vijaya's arrival. The controversy involves much more than a historiographical question, for deciding which community settled first has been important for the legitimation of the broader claims advanced for the land by the two peoples in contemporary times. The Sinhalese firmly accept their original North Indian connection and see themselves as Aryans, ethnically distinct from the Tamils who trace their ancestry to the Dravidians of South India. The terms 'Aryans' and 'Dravidians' do not stand up to close scrutiny and it is easy to dismiss both the claims of racial origin and racial purity maintained by the respective ethnic groups. However, they are central to the make-up of the respective self-identities of the two peoples.

Race is important but it has been the religious factor which has more profoundly influenced the shaping of the relations between the Sinhalese and Tamils. The religious division originated with the introduction of Buddhism in the 3rd century BC. Buddhism achieved spectacular success among the Sinhalese but it failed to make inroads among the Tamils, who remained Hindus. The embracing of the new faith by the Sinhalese did not result in their isolation from Hinduism and indeed, Hinduism was to make a noteworthy contribution to the development of the classical civilizations of the Sinhalese. Buddhism's greatest impact is to be found in ideological terms. This ideology was built around the special destiny claimed for the Sinhalese and the land they inhabited – at his *parinibbāna* (passing away), which significantly coincided with the arrival of Vijaya in the island, the Buddha had foreseen that it was in Sri Lanka that his religion would be protected – and it brought together land, race and religion in one unity. The principal vehicle which moulded the new ideology was the *Mahāvamsa*, the 'Great Chronicle' written in the 6th century AD (some scholars date it somewhat later). *The Mahāvamsa* presented a vision of a Sinhalese-Buddhist polity and this has strongly coloured not only popular thinking but also much of the historiography of the land. The Sinhalese-Buddhist ideology did not produce constant tension and conflict between the Sinhalese and Tamils. However, it carried great emotive power and this was demonstrated especially at times of political crisis. Thus, it was invoked against the invasions the Sinhalese kingdoms faced from the rulers and adventurers of South India and against divisive tendencies at the local political level during the period of the classical civilizations.

Later generations of Sinhalese have tended to dwell, not on the peaceful relations which were maintained between the Sinhalese and Tamils, but rather on the invasions from South India and the responsibility which the Tamils as an ethnic group should bear for the consequences. Over the years the following question has been asked again and again: were not the invasions responsible for the demise of the *rajarata* kingdoms and the eventual movement of the Sinhalese to the south-west leading to the abandonment of the heartland of the Sinhalese civilizations? The question is, of course, flawed for it fails to distinguish between the Tamil invaders from South India and the local Tamil population. The resistance which emerged on these occasions was glorified in the historical chronicles of the Sinhalese, and the heroes which the resistance threw up have carved special niches for themselves in the popular imagination. This ideology had its triumphs but its overall impact was limited: a political entity which could be described as Sinhalese-Buddhist was never sustained on an all-island basis. Moreover, the establishment of a separate Tamil kingdom in Jaffna in the early 12th century had important ramifications. The *de facto* situation made the claim of Sinhalese sovereignty over the entire island somewhat meaningless and it also enabled the Tamils to develop their own independent civilization and political organization.

Relations between the Sinhalese and Tamils were placed within a new framework with the establishment of European rule in Sri Lanka. The first two European powers, the Portuguese (1597-1658) and the Dutch (1658-1796), were attracted to the island because of its superb quality cinnamon – 'the Helen, or Bride in contest of this isle is the finest and purest cinnamon', the Dutch missionary Philip Baldaeus had written in 1672 – but they radically transformed the political landscape of the island by acquiring territorial power. The Portuguese began as rulers at Kotte, the first major Sinhalese kingdom of the south-west, by succeeding its last king who had bequeathed his throne to the King of Portugal. They expanded their power with the conquest of the kingdom of Jaffna in 1618 but were unable to gain control over the entire island: an independent Sinhalese entity in the interior, the kingdom of Kandy, successfully carried on the tradition of resistance to foreign power. The Dutch acquired the Portuguese territories after a bigger conflict, and although Kandy retained its independence, they were able to exact an important territorial concession in 1638 which made Kandy a landlocked kingdom.

The separation of the Sinhalese into two political entities resulted in a differentiation within the majority community: the Kandyans, largely isolated from the developments in the littoral and embracing the mantle of resistance to foreign power, began self-consciously to view themselves as being separate from the Sinhalese under European rule. On the other hand, although the Tamils and Sinhalese of the littoral were brought under a single dominant political power, the two ethnic groups were not treated alike either by the Portuguese or the Dutch. Indeed, the differences between the Sinhalese and Tamils were to be reaffirmed and emphasized. This was partly the result of deliberate policy: both powers consciously sought to exploit the differences between the ethnic groups to their political advantage. It was also partly due to the adoption of the view that the distinctive characteristics of the two peoples should be respected, if not for the sake of good order, at least for administrative convenience.

The rule of the first two European powers produced significant changes in the composition and structure of the local society. For example, the presence of the Burgher community, the descendants of 'pure' European marriages, or of marriages and liaisons between Europeans and mixed (Eurasian) or local women, dates back to this period. Never numerically large, the Burghers have historically been a powerful and visible social group. They have always been identified with European rulers – though the European-Burgher relationship was ambiguous in that Europeans did not treat them as fully equal – and their relationships with the local society have remained uneasily articulated.

Early European rule also led to the establishment of another community, the Christians, whose allegiance and loyalty to the country have at times been questioned because of extra-territorial relationships. The most readily identifiable Christian group consisted of Roman Catholics. The Catholics were the converts of Portuguese missionaries, the most zealous of the European missionaries, whose state-backed activities were distinguished by both proselytization and harsh persecution of the traditional religions. The missionaries won large numbers of converts but many reverted to their original faiths under the Dutch, though a significant hard core remained faithful, constituting the most important legacy of Portuguese rule.

Calvinism replaced Roman Catholicism as the established

religion under the Dutch, but missionary activity under their rule was much more restrained and less successful than that of the Portuguese. The Dutch treated the Buddhists less harshly, mainly in order to placate the Kandyan king, the guardian of Buddhist interests, whose cooperation was necessary to maintain the supply of cinnamon. The Hindus, who lacked an influential patron, won no tolerance, but it was the Catholics, who were viewed as the collaborators of the hated Portuguese enemy, who suffered the most at the hands of the Calvinists.

The Muslims underwent a significant transformation under the Portuguese and the Dutch. Descendants of South Indian trading communities who had embraced Islam, the Muslims came to the island as traders and had gained firm control of its export trade by the time the Portuguese arrived. The Portuguese, who saw them as their main trading competitors, adopted a harsh policy towards the Muslims. The Dutch moderated this policy but discrimination did not cease. The Dutch also promulgated a separate code of laws for them, as they did for several other social groups. The code was borrowed from Batavia – it was asserted that the Muslims were 'totally ignorant of what was, or what was not, their law' – and this exemplifies the crucial importance of the institutional devices developed by the Europeans in shaping the identities of the social groups of modern Sri Lanka.

The different social groups were thrown into an entirely new situation during British occupation (1796-1948), the last phase of European rule in Sri Lanka. The British too had first been attracted to Sri Lanka because of its valuable cinnamon but their eventual conquest of the Dutch territories was prompted by their imperial contest with the French which made it imperative for the British to gain control over Sri Lanka's strategically important Trincomalee harbour. The British were determined from the beginning to extend their power over the entire island. The elimination of Kandy did not come easily, but it was eventually achieved by a combination of military power and artful diplomacy which effectively exploited conflicts between the king and the Kandyan aristocracy. The cession of the Kandyan kingdom to the British by the Kandyan Convention of 1815 ended over three hundred years of Kandyan resistance to foreign power.

The littoral and the newly-conquered Kandyan territory were administered as separate territories until 1833 when a single government was created for the entire island. This was, in effect, a declaration that the strict parochial needs of a particular social group, or the pattern of settlement of different social groups, would no longer be the single most important factor in the administrative structure. The physical distances between settlement areas became less important with the rapid developments in communications, and the regional economies were gradually knitted together to form an all-island economy. Moreover, Western cultural influences began to spread more pervasively. These developments did not take place in a uniform fashion, nor did they fully succeed in countering forces which were throwbacks to the pre-colonial era. Nonetheless, British rule ushered in a framework within which there existed the potential for the different social groups to transcend their disparateness and to mould – as later 19th-century colonial writers articulated it – a truly 'Ceylonese nation'. Ultimately, of course, this was not to be, and indeed, the differences between the social groups were to be magnified by the end of British occupation.

The developments under British rule which affected Sri Lankan colonial society can be illustrated by focusing on four broad areas: religion, education, economy and politics. In the religious field, the new dimension was provided by Protestant missionary organizations. The Anglican Church became the established church but its primacy was challenged by other Protestant denominations, and sectarianism marred the activities of the Protestant missionaries throughout much of the 19th century. As a result, the Protestant community which emerged was deeply divided by allegiance to different denominations. Notwithstanding this, the new converts to Christianity were not divorced from the larger society from which they sprang. This can partly be explained by the absence of persecution, which in the past had powerfully bonded together indigenous converts. Furthermore, the position of the converts should be seen within the broader background of the more pervasive spread of Western culture; there were certainly aspects of the converts' behaviour which set them apart but there was also much which they shared with non-Christians who were influenced by Western values.

In the late 19th century the traditional religions began to react to the activities of the Protestant missionaries. The responses which occurred have been identified as revivalist movements, and they are important, not only because of the challenge they issued to Christianity, but also because they sharpened the self-images of the traditional religious groups. The most articulate and aggressive response came from the Buddhists of the low country.

Their concern was to safeguard their religion and to that extent there was a turning back to the past. However, the measures adopted to counter the missionary thrust were very modern in the sense that they were essentially imitative of Protestant methods and practices. The Buddhist response was multi-faceted, and it had the capacity to generate popular support. This activism was not without its internal contradictions but it testified to the inner strength of Buddhism. It should be noted that this was something which was hardly expected from a religion which was believed to have lost its vitality because of the withdrawal of the state patronage which had been so central to its functioning in the past.

In outlook and content, the Hindu and Muslim responses to the missionary activities were broadly similar to those of the Buddhists but they lacked the aggressiveness of the majority religious group. Nor were their activities broad-based. Both the Hindus and Muslims lacked a tradition of resistance to foreign intrusion which the Buddhists had inherited and which provided a vital dimension to their response to Christianity. Moreover, the Buddhists had a major grievance constantly before them: the failure of the British to abide by the guarantees made at the Kandyan Convention to 'preserve inviolate' their religion. On the other hand, the impact of the missionary activities among the Hindus was cushioned by the ability of the Hindus to draw support from their co-religionists in South India. The Muslims were the least affected by the proselytizing activities of the Protestant missionaries and their revivalism owed much to the leadership of a distinguished figure among them, the Egyptian 'Arabi Pashā, who had been exiled to the colony by the British after the suppression of his uprising in 1881-82.

The other important religious group, the Roman Catholics, were now free from persecution. The British attitude towards them was largely one of indifference. Aided by a devoted priesthood and efficient parochial institutions such as schools, the Catholics were able to develop a special identity centred around their faith, and in time they became one of the most cohesive social groups in the island.

Under the British, religion proved to be neither the sole, nor the primary, means of social mobility; the pre-eminent place occupied by religion during the rule of the first two European powers was now taken by education. The educational structure which was developed initially under the British was the result of a collaborative effort between the colonial government and

Christian missionary organizations, who viewed education as a significant feature of their mission of proselytization. The structure had sharply differentiated layers: a narrow level which offered an English education; and a broader level which provided 'vernacular education', instruction in Sinhalese and Tamil. The crucial importance of English education was that it was the key to securing social mobility and social status as well as wealth and access to goods and services so much valued by society. Not surprisingly, a high premium was quickly placed on English education.

The availability of an English education was narrowly circumscribed for it was distributed unequally. Since an English education was the *sine qua non* for entry into both the colonial administration and the professions in the later 19th century, the imbalance in the acquisition of an English education by the different social groups was necessarily reflected in the area of employment. The Burghers, who had adjusted remarkably well to the new reality of British rule, and the Tamils, who turned to outside employment because of the inability of land-based employment in their region to absorb an increasing population, were disproportionately represented, both in the government sector and in the professions. As in the Tamil north, English education came early to the Sinhalese littoral but its distribution was far more uneven, with the result that the opportunities it realistically offered in the populous south-west were relatively limited. The low-country Sinhalese increasingly challenged the primacy of the Burghers and Tamils in employment and among the Sinhalese community there emerged a grievance that it was disadvantaged educationally under the British. The Kandyans and Muslims were notably under-represented in employment. This was a reflection of the general lack of interest in English education shown by these two communities, whose dominant image was one of conservatism.

Given the rewards that could be reaped through English education and the visible successes achieved by Christians, it is not surprising that the revivalist activism of the late 19th century included a special emphasis on English education. The Buddhists, Hindus and, to a markedly lesser degree, Muslims, developed their own 'denominational' schools. These were largely imitative of the institutions established by the Protestant missionaries, and they did not dislodge the mission schools from their positions of primacy. However, they demonstrated that the traditional religions had the determination and resources, limited though they were, to challenge the Christians on their own ground. The new schools provided additional opportunities for English education, and they proved to be important channels for the reaffirmation of the respective identities and values of the religious groups.

The educational structure was responsible for the creation of a new social element, the English-educated élite. Recruitment to the new class depended solely upon English education; criteria which mattered for membership of other social groupings – race, religion and caste – were irrelevant. The new élite had much in common: a shared life-style, outlook and aspirations, and access to wealth, power and status. They were highly Anglicized, adopting Western dress, modes of speech and mores, and strove to achieve a goal advocated as early as 1801, that British policy be directed towards the creation of a class 'attached to their country by birth, and to England by education'. However, the homogeneity of the new élite proved illusory and their divorce from the local milieu was more apparent than real. The caste competition which arose among the Sinhalese in the last decades of the 19th century amply demonstrated that the narrow sectarianism of the old order continued to hold sway among those who claimed to hold a sophisticated world view. The leadership role taken by the new élite in the revivalist movements of the same period demonstrated that religious differences were not transcended by English education. The inherent lack of unity among the English-educated was exemplified most notably at the election for the 'Educated Ceylonese' seat in the Legislative Council in 1911, when the whole class was torn asunder by emotion based on caste and ethnicity. The increasing importance of ethnic divisions in nationalist politics was further evidence that the new élite's capacity to act as a distinct social group with common interests and values had severe limitations.

Although education was of crucial importance, it should not obscure the significant social impact the economy had under British rule. The new economy, centred on the plantation industry, was dominated by European interests, but the plantations in particular, and the economy in general, offered indigenous entrepreneurs unparalleled economic opportunities. There emerged an indigenous capitalist class, whose roots went back to the earlier European administrations. This new class had its internal contradictions, most notably the division along caste lines, which resulted from keen competition to exploit the new opportunities. The rivalry between the castes in the new economy sharpened the skills of the indigenous entrepreneurs as a group, and the continued dominance of Europeans in the economy legitimized not only their economic thrust, but also their eventual incursions into the political arena. The economic position of the new entrepreneurs was important but an English education remained essential if their social status was to be secured. Accordingly, they went to remarkable lengths to equip their children with an English education. Thus, important links were established between the new élite and the economy.

The vanguard of the indigenous entrepreneurship were the low-country Sinhalese and it was they who remained the dominant element in the new capitalist class. The traditionally pre-eminent caste in the Sinhalese littoral, the Goyigama, were best-placed to exploit the new economic opportunities but they were soon challenged by the conventionally lesser-ranked castes. These castes were less inhibited by the value-matrix of the traditional order and they proved to be more adventurous, establishing themselves in important economic spheres which were looked down upon by the Goyigama. Moreover, it was the low-country Sinhalese who also exploited opportunities in the Kandyan areas. The Kandyan Sinhalese in general spurned the new economy. It was not that they were insensitive to economic stimuli: there was a notable involvement of the Kandyan peasantry in the early stages of the coffee culture – the crop that ushered in the plantation industry in the 1820s – but they never fulfilled the promise they initially displayed. This failure has not been adequately explained. However, the effect of the failure is not in doubt: the economic success of the low-country Sinhalese aroused resentment and jealousy and this contributed to the emergence of a separate Kandyan consciousness.

Far more important in the evolution of Kandyan consciousness was the presence of another social group within their midst, the Indian Tamils. The Kandyan peasantry refused to become converted into a plantation work force and the British were obliged to turn to labour from South India. Sinhalese society has in the past displayed a remarkable capacity to absorb migrants from the neighbouring land without disequilibrium. Indeed, new castes were added to the Sinhalese caste hierarchy and migrants had been successfully assimilated in the immediate pre-colonial period. However, this pattern was not repeated with the Indian Tamils. The large numbers involved in the migration – which added a higher percentage to the total population than was added by natural increases – and the continued maintenance of strong links with their homelands, made the Indian Tamils different. The pattern of their settlement and the retention of their social structure and culture resulted in the creation of distinct social enclaves within the Kandyan region. The British social welfare legislation for the plantation workers and their manifest failure to adopt similar measures for the impoverished Kandyan peasantry made the Indian Tamils more than an irritant. They symbolized the adverse impact that the plantation industry had on Kandyan society. The Indian Tamils retained this stigma and became the victims of discriminatory legislation the moment political power passed to Sri Lankan politicians.

The role of the Sri Lankan Tamils in the new economy was of little more than marginal importance. They were involved in investments but no open competition resulted between them and the Sinhalese. The significance of this lies in the fact that when competition with economic implications developed between the two social groups in a different arena – in employment – it was of great intensity. Since they did not possess deep roots in the new economy, the Tamils were moved to guard zealously their achievements in employment.

Although some Muslims became entrepreneurs, they remained primarily as traders, and expanded their role by taking advantage of the changes that took place. The Muslim trader became a ubiquitous figure and his economic role was important both in the villages and in the urban areas. At the same time that their economic presence was becoming more dominant, the Muslims also began to act with a heightened self-awareness, primarily in the tradition of the revivalist activities of the late 19th century. The way these different factors converged to create overt hostility against them in the urban Sinhalese areas was dramatically demonstrated by the 1915 Sinhalese-Muslim riots, which were the first major incidents of ethnic violence in modern Sri Lanka.

The complex working of Sri Lanka's social plurality was remarkably displayed in the political arena during British rule. The antecedents of the nationalist movement which emerged in the first decades of the 20th century have been traced back, on the one hand, to the Kandyan resistance to foreign power and on the other, to the late 19th-century revivalist movements. Although it had the potential to take a mass agitational form, the nationalist movement primarily remained a movement led and controlled by an élite. Furthermore, its energies were almost singlemindedly devoted to achieving piecemeal constitutional advancement along the lines laid down for Crown Colonies in British imperial constitutional doctrine.

Sri Lanka's constitutional evolution can be traced back to the establishment of a Legislative Council in 1833. The legislature was designed to be the 'sounding board' for the Governor's formulation of policy, and its unofficial membership was so constituted that 'communal representation' became its hallmark from the beginning. Representation was first given to the Europeans, Sinhalese and Tamils, and by the end of the century it had been extended to the Muslims and Kandyans (the original Sinhalese member was henceforth styled the low-country Sinhalese representative). Furthermore, when the low-country Sinhalese representation was expanded, the selection was based on caste grounds, resulting in the appointment of a Goyigama and a Karāva representative, respectively. The officials were, of course, drawn from the English-educated and they were not preoccupied solely with the parochial interests of the groups they represented. Rather, what they sought was the agile balancing of 'national interest' with the safeguarding of their respective sectarian interests. Not surprisingly, in this they were not successful.

It was in the 1920s that the island's social pluralism truly came to dominate politics for it was at this time that the territorial elective principle emerged as the next stage in constitutional advancement. If the territorial principle replaced communal representation, then it was obvious that the numerical superiority of a particular social group would decide who would rule independent Sri Lanka. To the Tamils, Muslims and Burghers this meant the Sinhalese, to the Kandyans the low-country Sinhalese.

In the period following, the most unambiguous stance in politics was taken by the Burghers. They had been the earliest supporters of the British and had benefitted accordingly, especially in place-hunting in the administration. Despite their close links with the rulers, the Burgher leadership had emerged in the late 19th century to champion 'nationalist' causes. However, with others threatening to usurp their primacy, the Burghers steadfastly identified themselves with the British, which, of course, estranged them further from the other social groups.

An equally defensive role in politics devolved upon the Kandyans, for they had become disenchanted with their subordinate role in politics. Their position was clearly exposed when the elective principle was introduced. When the 'Educated Ceylonese' constituency was created, they formed only a minute percentage of voters (which also exemplified how far behind in

English education they were). Far worse, when a beginning in
territorial representation was made in the 1920s, it was the low-
country Sinhalese candidates who triumphed in the Kandyan
constituencies. The lesson was clear: the Kandyans were being
eclipsed in their own areas by the low-country Sinhalese, both
economically and politically. Thenceforward, the Kandyan
demand was to be unwavering; they sought the recognition of
their distinctive identity in constitution-making.

In order to gain constitutional concessions from the British,
there had been the closest political collaboration between the
low-country Sinhalese and the Tamils. This was exemplified in
the selection of a Tamil as the first president of the Ceylon
National Congress, that initial vehicle and symbol of the
nationalist aspirations of the English-educated. By the 1920s this
collaboration was to break down in the face of an acrimonious
dispute which centred on the safeguarding of minority rights
within a system of government based on territorial representation. This dispute also reflected an important shift in Tamil
perception: they no longer viewed themselves as a majority
community, to be bracketed with the Sinhalese – the reality was
that they were one of the host of minorities, though no doubt the
strongest. From this point the Tamils became an increasingly
inward-looking community, the affinities between them and the
Sinhalese were increasingly played down, and the ethnic
differentiations brought into sharper focus.

Caste as a factor of social pluralism remains to be reviewed.
Though they shared some common features, the Sinhalese caste
system was quite distinct from the Indian model, possibly due to
the impact of Buddhism. The very essence of the Sinhalese caste
system was its flexibility: there was no rigid stratification on the
basis of an immutable order of precedence of castes. This
flexibility has been demonstrated in a variety of ways: in the
transformation of caste ranking; changes in the functional role of
castes; and in the absorption of newer immigrant groups into the
caste hierarchy.

Traditionally, Sinhalese castes did not act with a fiercely
competitive spirit. There was ritual interdependence between
castes, and given that Sinhalese castes were of the 'functional'
type associated with landholding, the interdependence extended
to day-to-day conduct of economic activities. This is perhaps why
inter-caste regulations were so subtle and equally why caste
taboos and mutual caste avoidance did not cover the whole
gamut of social relations. This dimension was exemplified in the

absence of a category of 'untouchables' among the Sinhalese.

European rule introduced important changes in Sinhalese castes. Neither the Portuguese nor the Dutch saw the abolition of caste as a social goal. However, the policies pursued by them in several areas deeply affected caste. A case in point were the Salāgama, a lowly caste in the conventional hierarchy, whose caste occupations involving cinnamon earned them a special place in the economic policies of the Portuguese and the Dutch, as well as the early British. They were vested with extensive privileges and a whole institutional apparatus was created to maintain their caste exclusiveness in order to ensure their supply of labour. The Salāgama were geographically concentrated, and aided by their newly won privileges and importance, they developed a unity and an aggressiveness which were great sources of strength when they became free to compete openly in the economy. The new economic opportunities which opened up under the rule of the first two European powers enabled some castes to shift from their traditionally ascribed occupations. The classic example here were the Karāva, the fisher caste, who increasingly began to engage in trade and in activities requiring artisan skills. Such involvement outside traditional occupations gave castes such as the Karāva a head start over others when economic opportunities greatly expanded under the British.

The period of British rule brought about marked changes among the Sinhalese castes. A new economic framework, different from the one which had sustained caste in the traditional order, came into being. Caste was divorced from landholding, and the state no longer had an interest in maintaining caste. Thus, the Salāgama were freed of the fetters which had bound them to the state economy. In the new economy, opportunities became available regardless of caste status; caste identity and occupation were no longer inextricably linked together. Education introduced a vitally new avenue of social mobility and Western culture and values helped to dilute the norms of the old order. The ending of formal indices of caste, however, did not lead to the obliteration of caste identity in society; nor did the British abandon the consideration of caste in the formulation of policies. The most striking change which occurred was the replacement of caste interdependence by caste competition. This was as true of the economy as it was of social interaction. Thus, the conventional hierarchical arrangements of castes began to be increasingly attacked, as exemplified in the *'kara-goi* contest' of the late 19th century, which involved the challenge of the hierarchical primacy of the Goyigama by the Karāva. Not surprisingly, caste became a factor in politics. Thus, at the election for the 'Educated Ceylonese' seat of the Legislative Council in 1911, which involved a contest between a Karāva and a Tamil, the Goyigama voted almost *en bloc* for the Tamil candidate, moved by anti-Karāva sentiments. This not only indicates the importance caste achieved nationally, but also illustrates the complex threads that ran through nationalist politics.

The Tamil caste system was distinct from the Sinhalese system in that it more closely followed the Indian model. It had none of the flexibility of the Sinhalese caste system. Sacred sanction had an important place in the system and there were rigid distinctions between clean and unclean castes as well as between castes within the main classifications. As a consequence, the spatial distribution of castes within villages and inter-caste regulations assumed a greater meaning. The extent to which caste distinctions mattered in Tamil society was exemplified in the restriction of entry to Hindu temples to specific castes.

The Tamil castes were hardly affected by European rule – although given the impression that modernizing forces like education had upon the Tamils, this is indeed surprising. The reasons for this have yet to be adequately explored, though the close connection between Hinduism and the caste system at the practical as well as at the doctrinal level may be the explanatory factor. The consequence of this was that the hierarchical dominance of the Vellālas, who also held a commanding numerical superiority, was never effectively challenged by the lower-ranking castes.

If social pluralism was dominant in diverse sectors by the last stages of British rule, it is also true to say that independence dawned in 1948 with a great deal of optimism that divisive factors in society would retreat in the face of a commitment to a nation called 'Ceylon'. As negotiations were conducted for the transfer of power in the mid-1940s, there was a scramble, on the part of the minorities, to obtain safeguards against the impending majoritarian rule of the Sinhalese. The safeguards were enshrined in the constitution of 1948 – in the long run their effectiveness proved to be hollow – but equally important in the change in the climate was the recognition on the part of the Sinhalese leadership that concessions to minority concerns were a vital precondition for the granting of independence by the British. Independence was achieved with a spirit of accommodation and cooperation by all parties, between the British and the Sri Lankans as well as among the Sri Lankans themselves. This spirit was not to last long: the equilibrium achieved in 1948 under the British aegis by the competing political forces masked the reality that ethnic and religious claims and grievances were not unspent forces.

The task of charting the course for the new country fell upon D. S. Senanayake, who had led Sri Lanka to independence. Senanayake's political party, the United National Party (UNP), founded in 1946, won the 1947 general election and he became Sri Lanka's first Prime Minister. Senanayake intended his government to represent the moderate voice in politics and he was committed to a multi-racial and secular polity. His government was certainly broad-based but his commitment to a multi-racial polity was deeply flawed since one social group, the Indian Tamils, never found a place within it. In fact, the Senanayake government deprived the majority of the Indian Tamils of their citizenship and franchise rights in 1949. The only noteworthy opposition to this blatantly discriminatory legislation came from the Marxists, the principal political opposition to the UNP, whose vision of a multi-racial society was more sweeping than that of Senanayake. Senanayake's standing was also tarnished by his failure to dispel Tamil fears about possible discrimination under a Sinhalese-dominated government. He did win over the major political party representing the Tamil interests, the Tamil Congress, but a new party, the Federal Party (FP), founded in 1949, emerged to give articulate political expression to the Tamil fears.

The Sinhalese Buddhist majority also found no special niche in Senanayake's vision for his country. Few in 1948 saw the explosive potential which Sinhalese Buddhist opinion carried, but there was no doubt that the sense of injustice the Sinhalese Buddhists had long harboured about the fate suffered by Buddhism and its adherents under Western rule needed to be addressed with independence. It is arguable that, if the grievances of the Sinhalese Buddhists had been dealt with in the early years of independence, they could have been accommodated within the framework of the multi-racial and secular polity that Sri Lanka was proclaimed to be. As events turned out, the concept of a multi-racial and secular state became the casualty to sectional claims and counter-claims within less than a decade of the formation of the new nation.

Like D. S. Senanayake, Dudley Senanayake, who became

Prime Minister on his father's death in March 1952, did not give special consideration to the Sinhalese Buddhist claims. These claims had yet to find powerful political articulation, and the support of the community largely remained with the UNP. This was to change after Sir John Kotelawala succeeded the younger Senanayake as Prime Minister on the latter's resignation in October 1953. If the Senanayakes simply ignored the Sinhalese Buddhist claims, Kotelawala seemed to go out of his way, both in terms of his government's policies and personal behaviour, to offend the Sinhalese Buddhists. Kotelawala's tenure came at a time when there was a heightened self-consciousness on the part of the Buddhists because of the activities which were inaugurated to mark the 2,500th anniversary of the *parinibbāna* of the Buddha, which was to fall in May 1956. Moreover, there was now a viable moderate alternative to the UNP, the Sri Lanka Freedom Party (SLFP), founded in 1951 by S. W. R. D. Bandaranaike on his resignation from the UNP. Bandaranaike assiduously cultivated the Sinhalese Buddhist voter, and he was particularly responsive to the Sinhalese intelligentsia who were beginning to articulate and mould Sinhalese Buddhist opinion.

The growing sense of indignation which the Sinhalese Buddhists felt about the failure of the government to redress their grievances was compounded by the realization that, despite an electoral system weighted in their favour, the rural Sinhalese were excluded from the exercise of power. The lesson was patent: so long as the administration was conducted in the language of the last colonial power, the majority – who happened to be the Sinhalese Buddhists – would find no meaningful voice in governance. Thus emerged the issue which became the catalyst for organized political activity on the part of the Sinhalese Buddhists: the declaration of Sinhalese as the official language of the country.

The Tamil community was, of course, to react strongly to the developments which were taking place among the Sinhalese. The inward-looking tendency of the Tamils became more emphatic and the distinctiveness of the Tamils as a separate community became more self-consciously expressed, with their language both symbolizing and embodying this distinctiveness. The FP, with its advocacy of a federal constitution for Sri Lanka and of autonomy for the Tamil areas, became the vehicle through which the new sentiments began to be politically expressed. The FP's standing among the Tamils was unassailable, and without even the pretence of seeking electoral support in the non-Tamil areas, it became the most successful 'ethnic' political party in Sri Lanka.

The general election of 1956 saw the triumphant emergence of Sinhalese Buddhist populism as a political force. The UNP, which had failed to embrace the 'Sinhala only' platform until too late, was crushed by the Mahajana Eksath Peramuna (People's United Front – MEP), a coalition led by S. W. R. D. Bandaranaike whose populist platform gave primacy to the declaration of Sinhalese as the official language. In the Tamil areas a sweeping electoral victory was won by the FP. 'Ethnic politics' had come of age.

The new Bandaranaike government enacted legislation declaring Sinhalese the official language of the country in 1956. This law prompted a campaign of civil disobedience by the Tamils which in turn led to Sinhalese outbursts. The resultant 'race riots' demonstrated how fragile relations between the two communities would be in an emotionally-charged atmosphere. In the following year, Bandaranaike moved to make concessions to the Tamils and entered into an agreement with the FP, which *inter alia* provided for the recognition of Tamil as the official language for administrative purposes in the predominantly Tamil-speaking Northern and Eastern Provinces. The agreement (known as the 'Bandaranaike-Chalvanayakam Pact' after the two leaders) was vehemently and openly attacked with powerful elements within the MEP taking the lead, and it was hastily abrogated by Bandaranaike. Another race riot in 1958 revealed how vulnerable the Tamils were to Sinhalese mobs in the predominantly Sinhalese areas.

The failure of the 'Bandaranaike-Chalvanayakam Pact' raised the question of which precise terms and conditions would best satisfy the needs of the Tamils, and at the same time win acceptance among the Sinhalese Buddhists. The predominance of Sinhalese Buddhists in the polity at large was a reality with which the Tamil leadership was forced to contend. Equally, the Sinhalese leaders were conscious of the fact that concessions to the Tamils on their part could be exploited to their political discomfiture by their opponents. Interestingly, the failed 1957 pact became the basis for negotiation between the Sinhalese and Tamil leaders in the coming years. This was true of the negotiations that took place in 1960 between Sirimavo Bandaranaike (who took over the leadership of her late husband's party preparatory to the July 1960 general election) and the FP; and between Dudley Senanayake, who elected to lead the UNP again, and the FP prior to the 1965 general election. Mrs Bandaranaike's assurance that the 1957 pact would be implemented once she came into power proved illusory, and the agreement between the UNP and the FP that led to the FP participation in the new UNP government in 1965 soon collapsed without any meaningful achievement for the FP. As in 1957, in these instances, too, the Sinhalese leaders at the helm demonstrated a remarkable lack of political will to confront and challenge the opposition they faced from extreme Sinhalese Buddhist opinion which found any concession to the Tamils an anathema.

While the linguistic issue came to dominate politics from the mid-1950s onwards, there were other issues which had a profound impact on political relations between the different social groups. The 'Sinhala only' legislation was not the only tangible result of the newly-won primacy of the Sinhalese Buddhists; they were to benefit from their political thrust in other ways as well. The state, under Bandaranaike, extended its patronage to Buddhism generously, and the 2,500th anniversary celebrations of the Buddha's *parinibbāna* gave a special impetus to Buddhist activity. Despite the new attention which the religion received, the Buddhist community never doubted that Buddhism and its adherents were yet to recover the status and position they had lost during colonial times to the Christians and Tamils. The goal of securing for Buddhism the status of state religion continued to be pursued, and greater opportunities were sought for Buddhists in public life. There were demands that Buddhists should receive favourable treatment in recruitment as a way of ending the 'disproportionate' standing both the Tamils and Christians had in public sector employment. Further, Christian schools, which were seen to be the main agencies of continued Christian privilege, became the special targets of Buddhist activists. The government of Mrs Bandaranaike, in response to the activists, brought the Christian schools under state control in 1961, and the resistance to the measure by supporters of the Christian schools resulted in unprecedented tensions and conflicts between the Buddhists and Christians.

The predominance of ethnic and religious issues did not mean that the other historically important divisive force in society, caste, remained unarticulated in the post-independence era. Among the Sinhalese, caste rarely became the source of open conflict. Caste identity has been a key factor in the electoral behaviour of some conventionally lower-ranking caste groups, and allegations that caste plays a role in some areas of public sector recruitment have surfaced from time to time. Among the Hindus, the only noteworthy development was the faltering temple-entry movement which sought to end the prohibitions from temple entrance imposed on some low castes. Caste as a factor in politics received most attention in the activities of the Janatha Vimukthi Peramuna (People's Liberation Front – JVP). This ultra-left movement, which launched an insurrection against the Sirimavo Bandaranaike government in April 1971, attracted in the main the educated unemployed Sinhalese youth, and there is evidence to show that it was particularly successful among the young who perceived themselves as disadvantaged because of their lowly caste ranking.

Sinhalese-Tamil relations reached a new stage with the proclamation of a republican constitution in 1972 by the United Front government, a coalition of the SLFP and Marxists led by Mrs Bandaranaike, which won the 1970 general election. The new constitution, an autochthonous instrument which replaced the constitution of 1948 bestowed by the British, declared Sinhalese the state language and Buddhism the state religion. Sinhalese language now had constitutional rather than statutory recognition. The constitution was hazy on the status of the Tamil language, and the failure to explicitly clarify the constitutional standing of their language was a bitter blow to the Tamils. The newly-accorded status of Buddhism did not evoke protests on the part of most non-Buddhist communities – both the Christians and Muslims accepted it with equanimity – but to the Tamils this, together with the dismissal of their linguistic claims, signified and symbolized unequivocally their relegation into second-class citizenship.

The inauguration of the new constitution marked a crucial step in the long-drawn-out alienation of the Tamils from the polity at large. A separate state for the Tamils now became the goal for the community, since federalism, advocated by the Federal Party since 1949, was no longer a meaningful platform. The new goal found its political expression through the Tamil United Liberation Front (TULF), formed in 1976 by forging unity among the different Tamil political organizations.

The drive for separatism was spearheaded by educated Tamil youth who, by this time, had abandoned hopes for a future for themselves in a polity dominated by the Sinhalese. Above all, the 'district quota' university admissions policy, adopted in 1970, avowedly as a compensatory mechanism for the educationally disadvantaged rural students, but which heavily affected the intake of Tamil students into the higher educational institutions, symbolized to them the discriminatory intent and practices of the state. There was also an increasing estrangement on the part of the Tamil youth from the established political leadership of the community. It was evident that neither negotiations nor extra-parliamentary strategies such as civil disobedience pursued by the Federal Party had brought concessions from the Sinhalese. To the youth, the advocacy of a separate state was not simply a bargaining tool; it was a goal by itself, but one hardly likely to be conceded by the majority community through the democratic process. It is no surprise that the concept of an armed struggle became alluring to them. Thus, even before the TULF was formed to carry out the political struggle, there were already incidents of violence in the Tamil areas directed at both the state and Tamil supporters of the Bandaranaike government.

The separatist cause confronted not simply the Sinhalese Buddhists, who had been engaged in an on-going conflict with the Tamils, but all Sinhalese regardless of their religious identity. Separatism was vehemently rejected by the Sinhalese, not only because they were committed to the maintenance of the integrity of Sri Lanka, but because of their deep belief that their very future existence was now at stake. A separate Tamil state, so the argument ran, would constitute the first step in the creation of a greater Tamil state centred on Tamil Nadu in South India which wold eventually swallow up the Sinhalese people. Moreover, the Sinhalese were also disturbed by the links established between the Tamils and the Indian Tamils with the entry of the principal Indian Tamil political organization, the Ceylon Workers Congress (CWC), into the TULF. An agreement between Sri Lanka and India in 1964 had paved the way for substantial numbers of Indian Tamils to receive Sri Lankan citizenship (a larger number were to be repatriated to India, with the status of the remainder to be negotiated). Citizenship did not erase the image of the Indian Tamils as the 'unassimilated minority', and their new political links with those advocating separatism only heightened suspicions. The CWC's membership in the TULF did not last long – this demonstrated the considerable gulf which existed between the two communities – but the Indian Tamils continued to face Sinhalese hostility, and often became the victims of their anger, aroused by the separatist activity.

The general election of 1977 brought the UNP back into power with a crushing victory over the SLFP and the Marxists. In the Tamil electorates, the TULF emerged triumphant, and it saw the victory as a resounding endorsement of separatism by the Tamil community. This was questionable, for the opponents of the TULF and its platform, including the UNP, SLFP and the Marxists, garnered a substantial percentage of votes. The new UNP government, headed by J. R. Jayewardene, had full and ambitious plans, not the least of which was addressing Tamil grievances. The outbreak of widespread communal violence in August 1977 raised the question for the Tamils as to whether anything had altered. Certainly, the Jayewardene government took steps to reassure the Tamil community in the following years. Most importantly, the new constitution it fashioned and proclaimed in February 1978, which introduced an executive presidency to Sri Lanka, embodied several provisions designed to meet Tamil concerns, including the recognition of both Sinhalese and Tamil as national languages. The government was able to reap some political rewards – the CWC left the TULF to join it – but no critical breakthrough was achieved. The measures were neither adequate (Sinhalese, for example, continued to be the sole official language) nor comprehensive. What was abundantly clear was that the decisive voice in any settlement belonged to the Tamil youth, who had clearly lost faith in the political process. The commitment of youth to separatism remained steadfast, as did their belief that violence was the only way to reach their goal. The Jayewardene government in turn looked to its armed forces to put a stop to the violence in the north. The result was the increasing militarization of the Tamil areas.

The most decisive event in the growing deterioration of ethnic relations was the race riots of July 1983. The terrorist ambush of a routine army patrol in the north which killed thirteen soldiers was the immediate provocation of unprecedented Sinhalese mob attacks on the Tamils living amongst them. The government stood paralysed for days in the face of the refusal of the security forces to enforce law and order, and the accusation that powerful elements in the government itself were involved in organized attacks on Tamils, especially in Colombo, severely tarnished the leadership of Jayewardene. The experience alienated moderate Tamil opinion from the government, and it certainly gave new strength to the cause of the armed struggle for a separate state. The critical question in the aftermath of the events of July 1983 was whether the government had the will, capacity and opportunity to rebuild a polity which had become a shambles. It is a question which continues to remain unanswered.

Introduction

The bibliography

The present compilation has principally been guided by the general rubric established by the publishers for this series. As is inevitable, some deviation from the rubric was necessitated by the special features of the literature on Sri Lanka. Since the first English work on Sri Lanka was published in 1681 – Robert Knox's celebrated *An historical relation of Ceylon* (q.v.) – a vast literature on the country has appeared in the English language and indeed, as the distinguished bibliographer H. Á. I. Goonetileke has remarked, for its size Sri Lanka is the most written-about island in the world. Much of this, of course, does not merit serious attention. There is, however, a valuable specialized body of writings and it is this that has been primarily searched in compiling the bibliography. Where necessary, this has been supplemented by general and popular writings.

The literature considered for this compilation was extensive but the subjects it covers authoritatively are strikingly selective. Thus, while Buddhism has received detailed treatment, the other major religions – Hinduism, Christianity and Islam – have attracted relatively little interest within the scholarly community. As the reader will note, this imbalance is reflected in the bibliography. Specialized writings have appeared in the main in periodicals, though full-length writings are certainly not a rarity. Preference has been given to books and monographs but attention is also drawn to periodical articles where they constitute the only available writings on the subject, or where their special importance merits listing despite the availability of general studies. Highly technical writings have been ignored as have those which are idiosyncratic by nature, unless they have exerted a measurable influence. Finally, it may be noted that while the access of the Western reader to the material has been an important factor in selection, publications from Sri Lanka have found a central place in the compilation. Sri Lanka continues to have a remarkably thriving publishing industry in the English language and many writers, either by preference, or by necessity, publish in the island; no bibliographer can ignore the importance and value of this output.

What the reader is offered here is a select bibliography. For a fully comprehensive bibliographical treatment of the literature on Sri Lanka in the Western languages, the reader is referred to the multi-volume *A bibliography of Ceylon* (q.v.), the incomparable work of H. A. I. Goonetileke.

Introduction

Acknowledgements

I am grateful to the following who supplied material which was not available to me in the libraries I consulted and for their advice on the selection of entries: Devanesan Nesiah, Gananath and Ranjini Obeyesekere, Sid Perinbanayagam, Namika Raby, Sarath Rajapatirana, George Scott, H. L. Seneviratne, Stanley Tambiah and Gamini Wickremasinghe. To K. M. de Silva I owe a special debt for his sustained encouragement for my research over the years, including this compilation. Finally, if it had not been for the support and assistance I received from my wife Dineli and son Piyum, this work would not have been completed.

Chronology

c. 500 BC	Arrival of Vijaya, the legendary founder of the Sinhalese nation, and his followers from Northern India.
c. 300 BC	Founding of the Anurādhapura Kingdom by King Paṇḍukabaya.
250-210 BC	Reign of King Devānampiya Tissa. Buddhism formally established in Sri Lanka.
161-37 BC	Reign of King Dutugāmunu. Reconquest of Anurādhapura from the Tamil king Ḷāra.
992 AD	Capture of Anurādhapura by the Cōla emperor, Rājarāja I.
1017	Establishment of Polonnaruva as the new capital by the Cōlas.
1070	Overthrow of Cōla power and the establishment of the Sinhalese Kingdom in Polonnaruva by Vijayabāhu I.
1153-86	Reign of King Parakramabāhu I. Reunification of the Sinhalese polity.
c. 1190	Establishment of the Kingdom of Jaffna.
1215-32	Reign of Māgha, adventurer from Kaliṅga, at Polonnaruva.
1232-36	Reign of King Vijayabāhu III.
1236-70	Reign of King Parakramabāhu II. Dambadeniya established as the capital.
1272-84	Reign of King Bhuvanekabāhu I. Yapahuva established as the capital.

1341-51	Reign of Bhuvanekabāhu IV. Gampola established as the capital.
1371-1408	Reign of Bhuvanekabāhu V, the first ruler of the Kingdom of Kotte.
1469-1511	Reign of Senasammata Vikramabāhu. The establishment of the Kingdom of Kandy.
1505	Arrival of the Portuguese.
1521-81	Reign of King Māyadunnē, the first ruler of the Kingdom of Sitavaka.
1593	Reincorporation of Sitavaka in the Kingdom of Kotte.
1597	Philip I of Portugal becomes King of Kotte.
1618	Conquest of the Kingdom of Jaffna by the Portuguese.
1658	Dutch conquest of the Portuguese territories.
1796	British conquest of the Dutch territories.
1802	Treaty of Amiens confirms British possession of the Dutch settlements. Maritime Provinces declared a Crown Colony.
1815	Cession of the Kingdom of Kandy. Kandyan Convention signed between the British and Kandyan chiefs.
1818	Kandyan rebellion.
1823	Beginning of the coffee industry.
1830	Immigration of South Indian labour to plantations.
1833	Colebrooke-Cameron reforms: unification of the Maritime and the Kandyan Provinces, promulgation of new Charter of Justice, and establishment of Executive and Legislative Councils.
1848	Serious riots.
1860	Beginning of the tea industry.
1865	Municipal Councils of Colombo, Kandy and Galle established.

1869	Department of Public Instruction established.
1870	Ceylon Medical College established.
1874	Council of Legal Education established.
1880	Coffee blight brings the end of the 'coffee era'.
1910	Reform of the Legislative Council. Introduction of the elective principle.
1915	Sinhalese-Muslim riots.
1919	Formation of the Ceylon National Congress.
1920	Reform of the Legislative Council. Unofficial majority principle established.
1921	University College at Colombo established.
1923	Reform of the Legislative Council as a representative legislature.
1931	Establishment of the State Council under the Donoughmore constitution. Universal suffrage introduced.
1935	Formation of the Lanka Sama Samaja Party.
1942	University of Ceylon established.
1943	Formation of the Communist Party.
1944	Inauguration of universal free education scheme. Formation of the Tamil Congress.
1945	Soulbury Commission on constitutional reform.
1946	Formation of the United National Party.
1947	First general elections for independent Sri Lanka's Parliament. United National Party government formed under D. S. Senanayake.
1948	February 4: declaration of independence.
1949	Disenfranchisement of Indian Tamils. Formation of the Federal Party.
1951	Formation of the Sri Lanka Freedom Party.

1952 Dudley Senanayake becomes Prime Minister at the death of D. S. Senanayake.
Second general election. United National Party government formed under Dudley Senanayake.

1953 *Hartāl* (general protest strike). Resignation of Dudley Senanayake and his replacement by Sir John Kotelawala.
Bi-lateral trade agreement with China signed.

1956 Celebration of the 2,500th anniversary of the Buddha's attainment of *nibbāna*.
Formation of the Mahajana Eksath Peramuna.
Third general election. Mahajana Eksath Peramuna government formed under S. W. R. D. Bandaranaike. Sinhalese declared the official language.

1957 Transfer of British naval bases.

1958 Ethnic riots.

1959 Assassination of S. W. R. D. Bandaranaike. W. Dahanaike becomes Prime Minister.

1960 March: Fourth general election. United National Party government formed under Dudley Senanayake.
July: Fifth general election. Sri Lanka Freedom Party government formed under Sirimavo Bandaranaike.

1962 Legislation controlling mission schools passed.
Aborted coup attempt by military and police officers.

1963 Nationalization of the oil industry.
Communist Party (China) formed.

1964 Bandaranaike-Shastri agreement on the status of Indian Tamils.

1965 Sixth general election. United National Party-led government formed under Dudley Senanayake.

1966 Enactment of legislation for 'reasonable' use of Tamil in administration.

1969 Federal Party withdraws support from the government.

1970	Seventh general election. United Front government formed under Sirimavo Bandaranaike.
1971	April Insurrection of the Janatha Vimukti Peramuna. Abolition of the second chamber, the Senate.
1972	May 22: Republic of Sri Lanka established under new constitution. Enactment of the Land Reform Act.
1975	Nationalization of foreign-owned plantations.
1976	Formation of the Tamil United Liberation Front.
1977	Eighth general election. Formation of United National Party government under J. R. Jayewardene. August: ethnic disturbances.
1978	February 4: establishment of executive presidency with J. R. Jayewardene in office. May: proscription of Tamil separatist organizations. September 7: inauguration of new Republican constitution.
1981	Elections for District Development Councils.
1982	Presidential election won by J. R. Jayewardene. Extension of life of Parliament by Referendum.
1983	July: ethnic riots. Sixth amendment to the constitution banning political parties advocating separatism. Forfeiture of parliamentary seats by the Tamil United Liberation Front.
1984	All Party Conference on devolution and decentralization of power.

The Country and Its People

1 **Ceylon.**
Sinnappah Arasaratnam. Englewood Cliffs, New Jersey: Prentice-Hall, 1964. 182p. 2 maps. bibliog. (Modern Nations in Historical Perspective Series).
This retracing of Sri Lanka's history by a noted historian investigates the historical causes of the dilemmas which the nation faced in the post-independence era, and is valuable for the insights it offers on the interactions of the three major ethnic groups, the Sinhalese, Tamils and Muslims.

2 **Ceylon.**
Sydney Dawson Bailey. London: Hutchinson's University Library, 1952. 168p. map. bibliog.
Written for the non-specialist reader, this is a survey of the people of Sri Lanka and their history to 1948.

3 **Island Ceylon.**
Roloff Beny, John Lindsay Opie. London: Thames & Hudson, 1970; New York: Viking, 1971. 224p. map.
A magnificently and profusely illustrated book on the land, its peoples, their history and culture. The text is largely drawn from other writings on Sri Lanka.

4 **Sri Lanka: a survey.**
Edited by Kingsley Muthumuni de Silva. London: Hurst for the Institute of Asian Affairs of Hamburg, 1977. 496p. 6 maps. bibliog.
The collaborative work of eleven Sri Lankan scholars, this volume offers a comprehensive and authoritative overview of Sri Lanka. Part one provides background material, including coverage of geography, history and demo-

1

graphic trends. Part two is devoted to the economy, with essays on the economy in 1948, planning, foreign trade, industrial policy and agriculture. The statistical appendix to this part provides basic data on socio-economic conditions. Part three looks at political and constitutional developments, foreign policy and the administrative and judicial system. The final part deals with the cultural field – religion, education, literature and the arts.

5   **Modern Sri Lanka: a society in transition.**
Edited by Tissa Fernando, Robert N. Kearney.   Syracuse, New York: Maxwell School of Citizenship and Public Affairs, Syracuse University, 1979. 297p. 4 maps. bibliog. (Foreign and Comparative Studies/South Asian Series, no. 4).

In some respects the scope of this volume is broader than other recent collaborative work on Sri Lanka: apart from essays on political transformations, social change, economy, demography and education, the subjects of popular religion, the role of women, art and architecture, and Sinhalese literary traditions have been addressed. However, the focus of the essays is largely on the majority Sinhalese, and the failure to consider the minority communities in any detail has meant that the implications of the plurality of Sri Lankan society as regards the theme of transition have been considerably underestimated.

6   **An historical relation of Ceylon together with somewhat concerning severall remarkeable passage of my life that hath hapned since my deliverance out of my captivity.**
Robert Knox, edited by James Ryan.   Glasgow: James MacLehose & Sons, 1911. 460p. map.

Undoubtedly the most celebrated work on Sri Lanka, Knox's *An historical relation*, first published in London in 1681, is also the first book on the country to be published in the English language. Written by an Englishman who was held captive by the King of Kandy for twenty years, this account provides a sensitive and detailed description of Kandyan society and polity. It is an invaluable source for the understanding of traditional Sinhalese political and social organization, and should be on the reading list of every serious student of Sri Lanka. Knox's account has appeared in numerous editions. This edition by Ryan is noteworthy for its inclusion of the writer's autobiography.

7   **Sri Lanka. A country study.**
Richard F. Nyrop, Beryl Lieff Benderley, Ann S. Cort, Newton B. Parker, James L. Perlmutter, Rinn-Sup Shinn, Mary Shivanandan.   Washington, DC: American University, 1985. 5th ed. 523p. 7 maps. bibliog. (Foreign Area Studies).

Prepared in order to provide background information about Sri Lanka for United States government personnel, this handbook brings together useful data arranged under four headings, social, political, economic, and national security. The information is current up to May 1972. The first edition was entitled *Area handbook for Ceylon* and was published in 1971.

8 **Sri Lanka.**
   Urmila Phadnis. New Delhi: National Book Trust, 1973. 116p.
   bibliog. (World of Today Series).
   An introduction to Sri Lanka written specifically with the Indian reader in mind.

9 **India in Ceylonese history, society and culture.**
   Manayatt Dharmadam Raghavan. Bombay, India: Indian Council
   for Cultural Relations, 1969. 2nd rev. ed. 200p. 2 maps. bibliog.
   This study concerned with documenting India's influence on the culture and
   society of Sri Lanka suffers from the author's inadequate understanding of the
   historical developments of the country. The book was first published in 1964 (New
   Delhi, London: Asia Publishing House).

10 **The physical anthropology of Ceylon.**
   Howard W. Stoudt, based in part on data collected by J. R. de la
   Haule Marett, edited by P. E. P. Deraniyagala. Colombo:
   Government Press, 1961. 180p. 4 maps. bibliog. (Ceylon National
   Museums' Ethnographic Series, no. 2).
   This first (and yet to be superseded) monograph on Sri Lanka's physical
   anthropology is based on data collected during the Ethnographic Survey of the
   island conducted between 1937 and 1939. It includes a detailed discussion of the
   racial and inter-racial differences in the anthropometry and morphology of the
   people in the light of historical, environmental, and genetic factors.

11 **Ceylon an account of the island physical, historical, and
   topographical, with notices of its natural history, antiquities and
   productions.**
   James Emerson Tennent. London: Longman, Green, Longman &
   Roberts, 1860. 5th ed. 2 vols.
   Remarkable for the scope of the subjects it covers and the depth in which they are
   treated, this well-known study by a British scholar-administrator has retained its
   value as a standard work on Sri Lanka and its peoples. This was first published in
   1859 and quickly went through five editions, testifying to the popular reception it
   received.

12 **Ceylon: an introduction to the 'resplendent land'.**
   Argus John Tressider. Princeton. New Jersey: Van Nostrand,
   1960. 237p. map. (Asia Library).
   A survey of the island and its peoples, with the emphasis on description rather
   than analysis.

13 **The people of Ceylon.**
   Nanda Deva Wijesekera. Colombo: M. D. Gunasena, 1965. 2nd
   ed. 311p. bibliog.
   An attempt to provide a comprehensive understanding of the people of Sri

Lanka, covering a range of topics from their ethnic composition to food habits. There is much useful information but several subjects receive only superficial treatment.

14 **Twentieth century impressions of Ceylon; its history, people, commerce, industries and resources.**
Edited by Arnold Wright. London: Lloyds Greater Britain Publishing Company 1907. 916p. map.
This extensively illustrated work provides a valuable and fascinating picture of the colonial society at the turn of the 20th century.

The story of Ceylon.
See item no. 71.

A true and exact description of the Great Island of Ceylon.
See item no. 104.

Sinhalese social organization: the Kandyan period.
See item no. 113.

The historic tragedy of the island of Ceilao, dedicated to His Most Serene Majesty Dom Pedro the Second, King of Portugal, Our Lord.
See item no. 115.

François Valentijn's description of Ceylon.
See item no. 116.

Ceylon and its capabilities . . .
See item no. 121.

A view of the agricultural, commercial and financial interests of Ceylon . . .
See item no. 122.

A description of Ceylon, containing an account of the country, inhabitants and natural productions . . .
See item no. 125.

Ceylon at the census of 1911, being a review of the results of the census of 1911.
See item no. 126.

Eleven years in Ceylon, comprising sketches of the field sports and natural history of that colony, and an account of its history and antiquities.
See item no. 133.

Fifty years in Ceylon. An autobiography.
See item no. 153.

Geography

General

15 Ceylon, its geography, its resources and its people.
Elsie Kathleen Cook, revised by Karthigesapillai Kularatnam.
Madras, India: Macmillan, 1953. 360p. map.
First published in 1931 and long used as a school textbook, this work continues to
serve the reader who seeks basic geographical information about Sri Lanka. It is
divided into four sections – historical, physical, economic and human geography –
and is extensively illustrated.

16 An introduction to the geology of Ceylon.
Percival Gerald Cooray.   Colombo: National Museums of Ceylon,
1967. 324p. 2 maps.
As yet this is the only general work on the geology of Sri Lanka. The volume
incorporates research findings up to the mid-1960s; for subsequent developments
in the field, specialist journals will have to be consulted.

17 Handbook of the soils of Sri Lanka (Ceylon).
K.A. de Alwis, Christopher R. Panabokke.   Colombo: Soil
Science Society of Ceylon, 1974. 97p. map. bibliog.
A manual and guide to the soils of Sri Lanka, with discussions of both the macro-
and micro-regional differences. Includes a soil map.

18 **The agroclimate of Ceylon. A contribution towards the ecology of tropical crops.**
Manfred Domrös. Wiesbaden, GFR: Franz Steiner Verlag, 1973. 266p. 7 maps. bibliog.
The interrelationship between climate and agriculture – in particular tea, rubber, and coconut – is the subject of this monograph.

19 **Ceylon.**
Bertram Hughes Farmer. In: *India and Pakistan: a general and regional geography.* O. H. K. Spate, A. T. A. Learmouth, with the collaboration of A. M. Learmouth. London: Methuen, 1967. 3rd rev. ed. p. 786-824. maps.
This essay is a popular introduction to the physical and human geography of Sri Lanka. The discussion on the human geography is outdated but the material on physical geography can still be consulted with profit.

20 **Ecology and biogeography in Sri Lanka.**
Edited by C. H. Fernando. The Hague; Boston, Massachusetts: Dr. W. Junk Publishers, 1984. 505p. (Monographiae Biologicae, vol. 57).
This impressive collaborative work is the most comprehensive treatment available on Sri Lanka's ecology and biogeography. Its coverage includes geology, land forms, geochemistry, systematics and the ecology of faunal groups, the ecology of different habitats and of mammals, the role of ecological factors on parasitic diseases, and the impact of humans on the environment.

21 **Mineral resources of Sri Lanka.**
J. W. Herath. Colombo: Geological Sources Department, Ministry of Industries and Scientific Affairs, 1975. 72p. (Economic Bulletin, no.2).
An introduction to the subject, with the emphasis on the economically useful minerals.

22 **Sri Lanka. Land, people, and economy.**
Basil Leonard Clyde Johnson, M. Scrivenor. London; Exeter, New Hampshire: Heinemann, 1981. 154p. 100 maps. bibliog.
A competent review of Sri Lanka's environmental conditions and the development of its economy.

23 **The rainfall rhythm in Ceylon.**
George G. R. Thambyahpillai. Colombo: Colombo Apothecaries, 1955. 52p. (Climatological Research Series, vol. I).
The division of the climatic year of Sri Lanka into four seasons first offered in this work continues to be broadly accepted.

24 **The burst of the South-west monsoon: the new perspective.**
George G. R. Thambyahpillai. *University of Ceylon Review*, vol.
17, nos. 1-2 (Jan.-April 1959), p. 18-40.

An authoritative discussion of the onset of the major monsoon season with
reference to the large-scale weather forming factors which influence the climate of
the area in which Sri Lanka is located.

Sri Lanka: a survey
See item no. 4.

History of Ceylon.
See item no. 96.

Pioneer peasant colonization in Ceylon: a study in Asian agriculture.
See item no. 429.

Tea in Ceylon. . .
See item no. 435.

Atlases

25 **A historical atlas of South Asia.**
Edited by Joseph E. Schwartzberg. Chicago; London: University
of Chicago Press, 1978. 352p. bibliog. (Association for Asian
Studies Reference Series, no. 2).

Sri Lanka is treated in a comprehensive fashion in this work, with the data
ranging from its prehistory to the parliamentary elections of 1977. The
accompanying text provides explanatory material.

26 **Ceylon (Sri Lanka).**
Somasundaram Selwanayagam, Thambapillai Jogaratnam. In:
*World atlas of agriculture under the aegis of the International
Association of Agricultural Economists*. International Association of
Agricultural Economists. Novara, Italy: Istituto Geografico de
Agostini, 1973. vol. II, p. 65-73.

This text and its accompanying maps supplement and expand on the information
contained in the maps on Sri Lanka in the Committee for World Atlas of
Agriculture's *World atlas of agriculture under the aegis of the International
Association of Agricultural Economists: land utilization maps and relief maps
prepared by the Committee for the World Atlas of Agriculture* (Novara, Italy:
Istituto Geografico de Agostini, 1969).

27   **Sri Lanka economic atlas 1980.**
Sri Lanka. Department of Census and Statistics.   Colombo:
Department of Census and Statistics, 1981. new ed. 64p. bibliog.

First published in 1969 and now updated, this publication is intended to explain to the non-specialist the structure of the economy from the perspective of Sri Lanka's resources. Statistical tables, maps and explanatory texts are offered on the geographical background, climate, water resources, the people, plantation and peasant agriculture, industries, fisheries, energy and transport.

Travel Guides

28 **Insight guides: Sri Lanka.**
Produced and edited by John Gottberg Anderson.   Hong Kong:
APA Productions, 1983. 376p. 15 maps.

Intended for the 'second generation' traveller – the returning tourist who seeks
more than mere glimpses of the country being visited – this guide offers more
detailed information about Sri Lanka than is usually available in travel guides. It
includes short essays on Sri Lanka's geography, history, society and religion
written by specialists in the respective fields as well as information about places of
interest, festivals and pageants.

29 **The book of Ceylon, being a guide to its railway system and its varied
attractions for the visitor and tourist, with a description of Kandyan
architecture.**
Henry William Cave.   London: Cassell, 1912. Rev. ed. 664p.
5 maps.

A splendid example of the guide books that began to appear in the early 20th
century. Considerable information on the country is provided and the book is
amply illustrated with photographs. The chapter on Kandyan architecture is by
J. P. Lewis, a prolific writer on the culture of Sri Lanka.

30 **Ceylon yesterday – Sri Lanka today.**
Herbert Alexander Jayatilleke Hulugalle.   Colombo:
M. D. Gunasena; Stockholm: Stureförlaget AB, 1976. 247p.
7 maps.

Intended for the tourist, this work surveys the land, history, culture and places of
interest and is profusely illustrated.

31　**The footprint of the Buddha.**
Evelyn Frederick Charles Ludowyk.　London: Allen & Unwin,
1958. 182p. bibliog.
An elegantly written guide to the Buddhist monuments in Sri Lanka.

32　**Papineau's guide to Sri Lanka and Maldives.**
Singapore: MPH Magazines Pte, 1984. 214p. 5 maps.
The section on Sri Lanka covers culture, sightseeing, entertainment, sports,
shopping, and where to stay and eat. The work includes a street guide to
Colombo.

33　**Sri Lanka: a travel survival kit.**
Tony Wheeler.　South Yarra, Victoria, Australia: Lonely Planet
Publications, 1984. 3rd ed. 207p. 26 maps.
Aimed at the 'budget traveller', this guide offers basic facts about visas, exchange
rates, travel and accommodation costs, food and drink, health, the post and
telegraphs, as well as information about the different regions of the country which
are deemed worthy of interest to the tourist.

34　**Sri Lanka island civilization.**
Christian Zuber, Senake Bandaranayake.　Boulogne, France:
Editions Delroisse; Colombo: Lake House Bookshop, 1978. 212p.
Lavishly illustrated, with a text that seeks to evoke both tradition and modernity
in Sri Lanka and its peoples, this volume exemplifies the literature that emerged
in the 1970s to cater for expanding tourism.

Travellers' Accounts

35 **Eight years in Ceylon.**
Samuel White Baker. Dehiwala, Sri Lanka: Tisara Prakasakayo,
1966. 221p.

The famous explorer's account of travel in mid-19th-century Sri Lanka. The
original edition, entitled *Eight years wanderings in Ceylon*, was published in
London in 1855 by Longman, Brown, Green and Longmans.

36 **Golden tips. A description of Ceylon and its great tea industry.**
Henry William Cave. London: Sampson Low, Marston, 1900.
474p. map.

Primarily a celebration and an account of the tea growing areas. It is evocative of
the romance of tea and is a testimony to the significance the tea industry had
achieved by the turn of the century. Extensively illustrated with photographs.

37 **An account of the interior of Ceylon and of its inhabitants with
travels in that island.**
John Davy, introduction by Yasmine Gooneratne. Dehiwala, Sri
Lanka: Tisara Prakasakayo, 1969. 399p. (*Ceylon Historical
Journal*, vol. 16).

This account, by a doctor who served with the British army in Sri Lanka from
1816 to 1820, offers one of the first detailed views of the Kandyan region and its
people after the fall of the Kandyan Kingdom to the British in 1815. A valuable
historical source, the first edition of this work was published in London in 1821 by
Longman, Longman, Hurst, Rees, Orme and Brown.

38   Images of Sri Lanka through American eyes. Travellers in Ceylon in
the 19th and 20th centuries. A select anthology.
Compiled and edited by Henry Alfred Ian Goonetileke,
photographs by Yvonne Hanneman.   Colombo: United States
Information Service, 1976. 411p.

An anthology of travellers' accounts by Americans in Sri Lanka from 1813 to
1968. Twenty-three photographs supplement the text.

39   **Lanka, their Lanka. Cameos of Ceylon through other eyes.**
Henry Alfred Ian Goonetileke.   New Delhi: Navarang, in
association with Lake House Bookshop, Sri Lanka, 1984. 69p.

This slim but interesting volume presents first impressions of Sri Lanka recorded
by noted literary figures, including Pablo Neruda, Anton Chekov, Edward Lear,
Hermann Hesse, André Malraux, Christopher Isherwood, W. H. Auden and Paul
Bowles.

40   **A return to Kandy, Balana and beyond.**
Vesak Nanayakkara, drawings by Stanley Kirinde.   Colombo:
Arasan Printers for the author, 1977. 2nd ed. 256p. map.

A nostalgic evocation of the peoples, places and events of the Kandyan Kingdom,
the last Sinhalese kingdom which was ceded to the British in 1815. Illustrated with
line drawings by one of Sri Lanka's best known contemporary artists.

41   **Travels in Ceylon 1700-1800 by Wintergerst (1712) Ives (1773)
Guyard (1763) Falck (1767) de Jonville (1800).**
Translated and edited by Rowland Raven-Hart.   Colombo:
Associated Newspapers of Ceylon, 1963. 122p. map.

An interesting and varied collection of accounts by European travellers in Sri
Lanka during the time of Dutch rule. They provide fascinating glimpses of the
Dutch and of the people and the land they were ruling.

42   **Ceylon: history in stone.**
Rowland Raven-Hart.   Colombo: Lake House Investments, 1973.
2nd ed. 317p. map. bibliog.

An account of travel to places of historical significance, interwoven with
comments drawn from the descriptions of travellers who preceded the author.

43   **Island story.**
Jinadasa Vijayatunga, illustrations by Ivan Peries.   Madras, India:
Oxford University Press, 1949. 211p.

A beautifully written account of people and places of Sri Lanka which is
interwoven with the personal recollections of the writer.

**A description of Ceylon, containing an account of the country, inhabitants
and natural productions . . .**
See item no. 125.

Flora and Fauna

44   **A selection of the birds of Sri Lanka.**
John Banks, Judy Banks.   London: John & Judy Banks, 1980. 35p.
map.
A guide prepared for the general reader, with 192 species described and illustrated.

45   **Wild flowers of Ceylon.**
Dorothy Fernando.   Mitcham, England: West Brothers, 1954. 86p.
An illustrated guide to the more common wild flowers of Sri Lanka.

46   **A guide to the birds of Ceylon.**
George Morrison Henry.   London, New York; Bombay, India:
Oxford University Press, 1971. 2nd ed. 457p. map.
The best known guide to the birds of Sri Lanka, this work identifies and illustrates 400 species.

47   **The amphibia of Ceylon.**
P. Kirtisinghe.   Colombo: the author, 1957. 112p.
The standard work on Sri Lanka's amphibia.

48   **A history of the birds of Ceylon.**
William Vincent Legge.   London: Taylor & Francis, 1878-1880.
3 vols.
This classic study by a great ornithologist merits the attention of all serious students. The work appeared in three parts and includes thirty-four coloured plates and ten text illustrations.

49 **The behavior and ecology of the Asiatic elephant in Southeastern Ceylon.**
George Michael McKay.   Washington, DC: Smithsonian Institution Press, 1973. 113p. bibliog. (Smithsonian Contributions to Zoology, no. 125).

This study of the largest and best known mammal of Sri Lanka is based on the author's PhD thesis submitted to the University of Maryland.

50 **A guide to the freshwater fauna of Ceylon.**
A. S. Mendis, C. H. Fernando.   Colombo: Department of Fisheries, 1962. 160p. (Fisheries Research Station Bulletin, no. 12).

The first study to encompass the whole spectrum of freshwater fauna in Sri Lanka. The volume includes a listing of species.

51 **The marine and fresh water fishes of Ceylon.**
Ian S. R. Munro.   Canberra: Department of External Affairs, Government of Australia, 1955. 351p.

As yet this is the only detailed study on the subject.

52 **Manual of the mammals of Ceylon.**
William Watt Addison Phillips.   Colombo: Director, Colombo Museum; London: Dulau, 1935. 373p. map.

Extensively illustrated, this is the best known work on Sri Lanka's mammals and has retained its authoritative status.

53 **A handbook to the flora of Ceylon, containing descriptions of all the species of flowering plants indigenous to the island, and notes on their history, distribution and uses, with an atlas of plates illustrating some of the more interesting species.**
Henry Trimen.   Delhi, Dehra Dun, India: Bishen Singh Mahendra Pal Singh, 1974. reprint. 6 vols.

Encyclopaedic in scope, this classic, first published by Dulau and Company in London in 1893-1900, remains the standard work on the flora of Sri Lanka.

54 **The butterfly fauna of Ceylon.**
L. G. Ollyett Woodhouse.   Colombo: Government Press, 1950. 2nd ed. 133p. map.

A guide to identifying 242 species of butterflies in Sri Lanka. It includes 50 plates.

Ceylon an account of the island physical, historical, and topographical, with notices on its natural history, antiquities and productions.
See item no. 11.

Ecology and biogeography in Sri Lanka.
See item no. 20.

Coins and Currency

55   Ceylon coins and currency.
Humphrey William Codrington.   Colombo: Department of
Government Printing, 1975. 283p. (Memoirs of the Colombo
Museum, series A, no. 3).

One of the major achievements in the scholarship on Sri Lanka, this is the most
authoritative work on the subject. First published in 1924.

56   Ceylon currency–British period.
Benjamin Walter Fernando, foreword by Humphrey William
Codrington.   Colombo: Ceylon Government Press, 1939. 68p.

A survey of coins and currency issued by the British since 1796.

Prehistory

57 The late Stone-age of Ceylon.
Bridget Allchin. *Journal of the Royal Anthropological Institute*,
vol. 88, no. 2 (July-Dec. 1958), p. 179-201.

Attempts to present a coherent picture of the Stone Age in Sri Lanka on the basis of an assessment and synthesis of the literature on the subject.

58 Prehistoric Ceylon—a summary in 1968.
Siran V. Deraniyagala. *Ancient Ceylon*, no. 1 (Jan. 1971), p. 3-47.

A valuable summary of the published work on the prehistory of Sri Lanka, including an extended discussion of the Quaternary and the late-Stone Age culture identified as the Balangoda culture. The essay is extensively illustrated.

59 A theoretical framework for the study of Sri Lanka's prehistory.
Siran V. Deraniyagala. *Ancient Ceylon*, no. 5 (Jan. 1984),
p. 81-104.

This essay examines theoretical issues in the study of prehistoric Sri Lanka and considers in particular whether Sri Lanka should be viewed as an integral part of the southern or peninsular region which had an internal unity of its own in terms of material culture.

60 The physical anthropology of the megalith-builders of South India and Sri Lanka.
Kenneth Adrian Raine Kennedy. Canberra: Australian National University, 1975. 94p. bibliog.

A synthesis of the research and writings on the physical anthropology and palaeodemography of the megalith-builders of Sri Lanka.

Prehistory

61 **Pre-historic archeology in Ceylon.**
   S. P. F. Senaratne.   Colombo: Department of National Museums,
   1969. 45p. (Ceylon National Museums Handbooks, Series – 2).
An introduction to the methodology of prehistoric archaeology in Sri Lanka. The
author also surveys the major findings in the field.

History of Ceylon.
See item no. 96.

Archaeology
and Epigraphy

62 **The story of Ceylon archaeology.**
Don Titus Devendra.   Colombo: Archaeological Society of Ceylon,
1969. 30p.
A useful survey of the developments in the field of archaeology in Sri Lanka.

63 **Ancient inscriptions in Ceylon.**
Edward Müller.   London: Trubner, 1883. 2 vols.
The first edition of inscriptions to be published in monograph form, this volume
contains 172 inscriptions with translations.

64 **Inscriptions of Ceylon, vol. 1, containing cave inscriptions from 3rd
century B.C. to 1st century A.C. and other inscriptions in the early
Brahmi script.**
Senarat Paranavitana.   Colombo: Department of Archaeology,
1970. 163p. map.
The first volume of a corpus of Sri Lanka inscriptions planned by the author
which was left unfinished at his death in 1972. There is a lengthy introduction
which analyses the inscriptions and evaluates their value for the study of early
history.

65 **Glimpses of Ceylon's past.**
Senarat Paranavitana.   Colombo: Lake House Investments, 1972.
199p. map.
A collection of extracts of the *Annual Reports* of the Archaeological Survey of Sri
Lanka for 1940-56, the period during which the author was the Commissioner of
Archaeology. It provides the reader with a valuable insight into archaeological
discoveries and research during one of the most important periods of the Survey.

66 **Ceylon Tamil inscriptions.**
   Edited by A. Velupillai.   Peradeniya, Sri Lanka: the author,
   1971-72. 2 parts.
An attempt to bring together and critically review the Tamil inscriptions of Sri
Lanka. Fifty-seven inscriptions are examined in these volumes.

A short history of Ceylon.
See item no. 67.

Sinhalese monastic architecture: the viharas of Anurādhapura.
See no. item 512.

Senarat Paranavitana commemoration volume.
See item no. 530.

Epigraphia Zeylanica, being lithic and other inscriptions of Ceylon.
See item no. 572.

Epigraphical Notes.
See item no. 573.

History

General

67 A short history of Ceylon.
Humphrey William Codrington, with a chapter on archaeology by
Arthur Maurice Hocart.   London: Macmillan 1947. 202p. 7 maps.
The best known short history of Sri Lanka, this work, first published in 1926 and
revised in 1939, remains worthy of attention, even though it is outdated in some
respects.

68 A history of Sri Lanka.
Kingsley Muthumuni de Silva.   London: C. Hurst; Berkeley,
California; Los Angeles: University of California Press; New Delhi:
Oxford University Press, 1982. 603p. bibliog.
The history of Sri Lanka from its beginnings in the 5th century BC to the major
realignment of contemporary Sri Lanka's political forces that took place at the
general election of 1977 is traced in this study. An epilogue brings the story up to
May 1981. Reflecting the author's expertise and the state of historiography, the
account emphasizes the period of British rule and political events and movements.
However, other major themes are not ignored and there is in fact considerable
information about economic conditions and social structures and social change.
This is the best one-volume history of Sri Lanka currently available.

69 **Ceylon.**
Karunadasa Wijesiri Goonewardena. In: *The historiography of the British Empire – Commonwealth: trends, interpretations and resources*. Edited by Robin W. Winks. Durham, North Carolina: Duke University Press, 1966, p. 421-47.

This examination of the primary sources for the study of the history of Sri Lanka and critical review of the major historical writings is an admirable introduction to the historiography of Sri Lanka.

70 **List of tombstones and monuments in Ceylon, of historical and local interest, with an obituary of persons undocumented.**
John Penry Lewis. Colombo: Government Printer, 1913. 462p.

This is an unusual and exceedingly valuable source of information on the European community in Sri Lanka, both official and unofficial.

71 **The story of Ceylon**
Evelyn Frederick Charles Ludowyk. London: Faber, 1967. 2nd ed. 236p. 2 maps. bibliog.

An elegant survey of historical developments, written from the perspective of one who looks back to the past of Sri Lanka in order to find clues for the understanding of the country in the late 1960s. An American edition of this work is also available: *A short history of Ceylon* (New York; Washington, DC: Praeger, 1967. 336p. 2 maps. bibliog.).

72 **Ceylon today and yesterday; main currents of Ceylon history.**
Garrett Champness Mendis. Colombo: Associated Newspapers of Ceylon, 1963. 2nd rev. ed. 228p. 6 maps. bibliog.

A thematic treatment of Sri Lanka's history by the well-known historian.

73 **Ceylon.**
Sydney Arnold Pakeman. London: Benn, 1967. 256p. map. bibliog. (Nations of the Modern World Series).

A lucidly written historical survey, with the greater part of the book devoted to the British in Sri Lanka. The author's concern with defending the British record colours his interpretations.

74 **Sri Lanka: a handbook of historical statistics.**
Patrick Peebles. Boston, Massachusetts: G. K. Hall, 1982. 357p. (A Reference Publication In International Historical Statistics).

The data, drawn from official publications, is arranged under broad categories; most of it relates to the 20th century, though there is data for the 19th century in some categories. The crucial question of whether the data is reliable does not receive proper treatment. Nor has the compiler adequately considered another major problem faced by those using historical statistics, namely the reconciliation of differences between sets of official data covering the same subject matter.

75   **A Marxist looks at the history of Ceylon.**
Nagalingam Sanmugathasan.   Colombo: Sarasavi Printers, 1974.
2nd ed. 101p.
A provocative extended essay by the General Secretary of the Communist Party
(China), who has long been a leading figure in the Leftist movement in Sri Lanka.
It exemplifies the doctrinaire Marxist approach to Sri Lanka's history.

76   **Sri Lanka in transition.**
W. M. Karunaratne Wijetunga.   Colombo: Wesley Press, 1974.
146p. 2 maps. bibliog.
An academic historian's survey of Sri Lanka's history. The more recent
developments are reviewed from the standpoint of an active participant.

77   **Ceylon: between Orient and Occident.**
Zeylanicus [pseud.], foreword by Sydney Arnold Pakeman.
London: Elek Books, 1970. 288p. 3 maps. bibliog.
A history of Sri Lanka up to the general election of 1970, with greater attention
devoted to British rule. The reader may well be struck by the author's sentimental
attachment to the British.

Historical chronicles

78 **Cūlavaṃsa being the more recent part of the Mahavamsa.**
    Translated by Wilhelm Geiger and from the German into English by
    C. Mabel Rickmers. Colombo: Ceylon Government Information
    Department, 1953. 2 parts.

The first part of this Pāli chronicle (known as *Cūlavaṃsa* I) is attributed to
Dhammakitti, a Buddhist monk who lived in the 13th century, and surveys the
island's history to the end of the 12th century. The second part (*Cūlavaṃsa* II)
was written in the 14th century by an unknown monk and continues the story up
to the early 14th century, and the final part (*Cūlavaṃsa* III), the work of an
unknown monk of the 19th century, carries the story forward to the fall of the last
Sinhalese kingdom to the British in 1815. Though less influential than the
Mahāvaṃsa in moulding the Sinhalese-Buddhist identity, this chronicle has
proved to be an invaluable source to historians. Taken together, the *Mahāvaṃsa*,
and its continuation, *Cūlavaṃsa*, testify to the remarkable tradition of historical
writing among the Sinhalese.

79 **Mahāvamsa or the great chronicle of Ceylon.**
    Translated by Wilhelm Geiger, assisted by Mabel Haynes Bode,
    with an addendum by Garrett Champness Mendis. London: Pali
    Text Society, 1980. 323p. map. (Pali Text Society Translation
    Series, no. 3).

The foremost of the Pāli chronicles, this work was written in the 6th century (the
exact date is still subject to controversy) by Mahānāma, a Buddhist monk. It gives
a detailed account of the religious and political history of Sri Lanka from the
arrival (some time in the 5th century BC) in the island of the legendary founding
father of the Sinhalese people, Vijaya, from northern India. It is the major
historical source for ancient Sri Lanka. More important, with its close
intertwining of national identity with Buddhism in its historical interpretations,
this work has exerted a powerful influence over the Sinhalese, an influence which
very soon took on ideological dimensions. This translation, by the best known
authority on the historical chronicles, was first published in 1908.

80 **Historical writing in Sinhalese.**
    Charles Edmund Godakumbura. In: *Historians of India, Pakistan
    and Ceylon*. Edited by C. H. Philips. London: Oxford University
    Press, 1961, p. 72-86.

A critical review of the Sinhalese chronicles and other Sinhalese historical writings
up to the end of the 19th century.

81   **The Rājāvāliya, or a historical narrative of Sinhalese kings from Vijaya to Vimala Dharma Suriya II.**
Edited by B. Gunasekara.   Colombo: Government Printer, 1954.
88p.
The most important of the Sinhalese chronicles, this work by an unknown author, is a narrative of the events, mainly political, which occurred during the successive reigns of kings up to the end of the 17th century. As a historical source, this chronicle ranks next to the *Mahāvaṃsa*.

82   **The Dīpavamsa: an ancient Buddhist historical record.**
Edited and translated by Hermann Oldenberg.   New Delhi: Asian Educational Services, 1982. 227p.
The oldest surviving Pāli chronicle, this work was compiled in the early 4th century. It surveys the history of Sri Lanka to the end of the 3rd century. This translation, first published by Williams and Norgate in London in 1879, is acknowledged to be the most authoritative.

83   **The Pāli chronicles of Ceylon.**
Lakshman S. Perera. In: *Historians of India, Pakistan and Ceylon.*
Edited by C. H. Philips.   London: Oxford University Press, 1961,
p. 29-43.
A critical examination of the Pāli chronicles which can be used as an introduction to the major sources historians depend on for the study of the early history of Sri Lanka.

Early history of Buddhism in Ceylon: or 'state of Buddhism in Ceylon as revealed by the Pali commentaries of the 5th century A.D.'
See item no. 84.

Culture of Ceylon in mediaeval times.
See item no. 88.

The two wheels of dhamma: essays on the Theravada tradition in India and Ceylon.
See item no. 214.

Religion and legitimation of power in Sri Lanka.
See item no. 216.

Classical civilizations

84 **Early history of Buddhism in Ceylon: or 'state of Buddhism in Ceylon as revealed by the Pali commentaries of the 5th century A.D.'**
E. W. Adikaram. Colombo: Ceylon Daily News Press, 1946. 154p. bibliog.

This study is narrower in scope than many other histories but nonetheless continues to be cited as an authoritative work on the history of Buddhism up to the 5th century.

85 **Society in mediaeval Ceylon.**
Manikka Badatura Ariyapala. Colombo: Department of Cultural Affairs, 1968. 2nd ed. 415p. map. bibliog.

The published version of a London University PhD thesis, this is a study of the polity and society of 13th-century Sri Lanka, which uses contemporary Sinhalese literary works as the primary sources.

86 **Ancient irrigation works in Ceylon.**
Richard Leslie Brohier. Colombo: Ministry of Mahavali Development, 1979. 157p. 43 maps.

Originally published in three parts in 1934-35, this volume offers detailed historical and technical information relating to the irrigation works of the classical civilizations.

87 **Social history of early Ceylon.**
Hema Ellawala. Colombo: Department of Cultural Affairs, 1969. 191p. bibliog.

The social institutions of the period from the 5th century BC to 4th century AD are examined, with particular attention given to the transformation that took place in the Hindu-influenced institutions after the introduction of Buddhism in the 3rd century AD. This study is based on the author's London University PhD thesis.

88 **Culture of Ceylon in mediaeval times.**
Wilhelm Geiger, edited by Heinz Bechert. Wiesbaden, GFR: Otto Harrassowitz, 1960. 286p. map. bibliog.

Posthumously published, this work incorporates the remarkable scholarship of the German Indologist who played a seminal role in the study of classical civilizations of Sri Lanka. Drawing on the historical chronicles, mainly the *Mahāvaṃsa*, Geiger examines the geographical background, the people, king and government, and religion and church. The appendixes present the author's previously unpublished corrections to the historical chronicles, *Mahāvaṃsa* and *Cūlavaṃsa*.

89   **Tamils of Sri Lanka. Their history and role.**
P.A.T. Gunasinghe.   Colombo: H. W. Cave, [1985]. 125p. 3 maps.

The settlement patterns of Tamils in the island from the earliest times, their role in political history and the creation of the Kingdom of Jaffna are discussed in this study. The author, using an impressive range of sources, challenges the conclusions drawn in S. Pathmanathan's *Kingdom of Jaffna* (q.v.) about the origins and establishment of the Jaffna Kingdom, an issue of considerable importance in contemporary Sinhalese-Tamil relations. However, Gunasinghe's polemical tone mars his argument.

90   **Irrigation and hydraulic society in early medieval Ceylon.**
R. A. L. H. Gunawardana.   *Past and Present*, no. 53 (Nov. 1971), p. 3-27.

An examination of the structure and organization of the society, polity and economy of the classical civilizations, in order to establish that the theory of 'Oriental despotism' advanced by Karl Wittfogel does not fit the Sri Lankan case. The author's discussion of the structure which evolved for the construction and maintenance of irrigation works is particularly illuminating.

91   **Robe and plough: monasticism and economic interest in early medieval Sri Lanka.**
R. A. L. H. Gunawardana.   Tucson, Arizona: University of Arizona Press, 1979. 377p. 3 maps. bibliog. (Association for Asian Studies Monograph, no. 35).

This study, which broke new ground in the interpretation of the early history of Sri Lanka, is devoted to an examination of the agriculture-based polity and society of the classical times. Particularly penetrating are the chapters on monastic property and their management, which reveal the crucial role played by the powerful monasteries in the economy. The study also examines the structural organization of the priesthood and the changes it underwent, its rituals and cults, and the interaction of Sri Lankan Buddhist centres with those overseas. This is a revised version of the author's London University doctoral dissertation.

92   **History of kingship in Ceylon up to the fourth century A.D.**
Tilak Hettiarachchy.   Colombo: Lake House Investments, 1972. 208p. map. bibliog.

The nature and function of the institution of kingship, an important issue in the historiography of early Sri Lanka, is examined in this study. This is the revised version of the author's London University doctoral dissertation.

93   **The collapse of the Rajarata civilization in Ceylon and the drift to the south-west.**
Edited by Karthigesu Indrapala.   Peradeniya, Sri Lanka: Ceylon Studies Seminar, 1971. 126p. bibliog.

The eight essays in this collection address a major historiographical issue in the early history of Sri Lanka, why did the civilization centred on Polonnaruva collapse and the population shift permanently to the southwest? Some of the essays have been published before, while others appear in print for the first time (most of these draw upon material in unpublished doctoral dissertations). The essays, with their divergent and often conflicting interpretations, testify to the complexity of the issue.

94　**The decline of Polonnaruwa and the rise of Dambadeniya.**
Amaradasa Liyanagamage.　Colombo: Department of Cultural Affairs, 1968. 213p. map. bibliog.

The factors that led to the shift of the political capital of the Sinhalese kingdom from Polonnaruva to Dambadeniya, which marked the beginning of the development identified in historiography as the 'drift to the south-west', is the subject of this published version of the author's London University PhD thesis.

95　**The early history of Ceylon, and its relations with India and foreign countries.**
Garrett Champness Mendis.　New York: AMS Press, 1975. 103p. 3 maps.

This is a reprint of the 1932 edition of a once widely used text book. It may still be usefully consulted for general historical outlines.

96　**History of Ceylon.**
Edited by Senarat Paranavitana.　Colombo: Ceylon University Press Board, 1959, 1960. 2 parts. (University of Ceylon History of Ceylon, vol. 1, parts I & II).

A collective attempt to provide a comprehensive treatment of the history of Sri Lanka from its beginnings to the arrival of the Portuguese in 1505. This work examines in detail the geographical background, prehistory, historical sources, political developments, religion and culture. The authoritative standing of the work has been considerably diminished by research conducted subsequent to its publication.

97　**The Kingdom of Jaffna, part I (circa. 1250-1450).**
Sivasubramaniam Pathmanathan.　Colombo: Rajendra Press, 1978. 302p. map. bibliog.

This study deals with the background to and the establishment of the Kingdom of Jaffna, the first independent political entity of the Tamils. The author thus addresses an important historiographical issue – parenthetically, it may be noted that this issue has also attracted considerable public attention contemporaneously in the context of Sinhalese-Tamil relations. The study is based on the author's London University PhD thesis.

98   **History of Buddhism in Ceylon. The Anurādhapura period, 3rd
      century BC-10th century AC.**
      Walpola Rahula.   Colombo: M.D. Gunasena, 1966. 2nd ed. 351p.
      2 maps. bibliog.
The standard work on the introduction of Buddhism to Sri Lanka and its early
development, with an extended discussion of monasticism.

99   **Sri Lanka and South-East Asia: political, religious and cultural
      relations from A.D. c.1000 to c.1500.**
      W. M. Sirisena.   Leiden, The Netherlands: Brill, 1978. 186p.
      bibliog.
An overarching view of Sri Lanka's relations with Southeast Asia during an
important period in its history, which argues that these relations were as
important as its relations with the Indian sub-continent.

100   **The political history of the kingdom of Kotte 1400-1521.**
      Gintota Parana Vidanage Somaratne.   Gangodawila, Sri Lanka:
      Deepani Printers, 1975. 362p. 2 maps. bibliog.
The published version of the author's London University doctoral dissertation,
this is the most detailed treatment currently available on the principal Sinhalese
kingdom of the 15th century.

101   **Historical topography of ancient and mediaeval Ceylon.**
      Cyril Wace Nicholas.   *Journal of the Ceylon Branch of the Asiatic
      Society*, new series, vol. 6 (1959), p. 1-223.
This painstakingly researched monograph, issued as a special number of the
leading journal, discusses historical topography from the earliest times to the end
of the 13th century, with references made to modern territorial arrangements.

Religion and legitimation of power in Sri Lanka.
See item no. 216.

Ancient land tenure and revenue in Ceylon.
See item no. 410.

Land tenure and revenue in mediaeval Ceylon (A.D. 1000-1500).
See item no. 419.

Sinhalese monastic architecture: the viharas of Anurādhapura.
See item no. 512.

Western powers and the indigenous kingdoms (1505-1796)

102 **Portuguese rule in Ceylon, 1594-1612.**
Tikiri Abeyasinghe.   Colombo: Lake House Investments, 1966.
247p. 3 maps. bibliog.

This study, originally a PhD dissertation submitted to the University of London, examines the coming of the Portuguese to Sri Lanka and the establishment and expansion of their rule in the littoral. Its discussion of the complex interaction of the foreign power with the indigenous rulers is particularly valuable. The structure of the Portuguese administration, missionary activities and the impact of Portuguese rule are also examined in detail.

103 **Dutch power in Ceylon (1658-1687).**
Sinnappah Arasaratnam.   Amsterdam: Djambatan, 1958. 256p.
2 maps. bibliog.

An important account which examines the consolidation of Dutch rule in the littoral of Sri Lanka. The political relations of the Dutch with the Kandyan king and the Kingdom of Jaffna, their military activities in the littoral and against Kandy, their economic organization and cultural impact receive extended treatment. One of the first studies to use the archives at the Hague extensively, this is the published version of a London University doctoral dissertation.

104 **A true and exact description of the Great Island of Ceylon.**
Philip Baldaeus, translated by Pieter Brohier, with an introduction by S. D. Saparamadu.   Colombo: Royal Asiatic Society (Ceylon Branch), 1960. 403p; *Ceylon Historical Journal*, vol. 8, nos. 1-4 (July 1958-April 1959).

This work, first published in Dutch in Amsterdam in 1672, was authored by a Dutch missionary who came to Sri Lanka at the time of the expulsion of the Portuguese by the Dutch and remained there until 1665 leading the Dutch proselytising efforts among the local population. Baldaeus provides detailed information about the land and its people, and critically considers the Dutch rulers and their policies. The work is an invaluable source for the study of the Dutch rule in the island in the 17th century.

105 **The Catholic Church in Ceylon under Dutch rule.**
Robrecht Boudens.   Rome: Officium Libri Catholici, 1957. 266p.
2 maps. bibliog.

Examines the trials of the Catholic Church during the period of Dutch rule, when it lost the favoured position it had enjoyed under the previous Western rulers, the Portuguese. While the change in the Church's fortunes under the Dutch is effectively brought out, the author exaggerates the persecution Catholics faced under the Dutch.

106 **The Portuguese rule in Ceylon, 1617-1638.**
Chandra Richard de Silva.   Colombo: H. W. Cave, 1972. 267p.
map. bibliog.

The period when the rule of the Portuguese was at its most powerful is the focus of this important study. Using both Portuguese and Sinhalese sources, the author explores Portuguese-Kandyan relations, the development of the Portuguese administrative structure, economic conditions, treatment of the indigenous peoples, and Catholic missionary undertakings. This is the revised version of the author's London University doctoral dissertation.

107 **A study of the political, administrative and social structure of the Kandyan kingdom of Ceylon, 1707-1760.**
Lorna Srimathie Dewaraja.   Colombo: Lake House Investments, 1972. 245p. 2 maps. bibliog.

The rule of the Nayakkars, the efforts of this dynasty of South Indian origin to legitimize itself and the tensions and conflicts that arose between them and the Kandyan aristocracy form the major part of this study. The administrative and social structure of the kingdom is also examined but the discussion is marred by the use of questionable sources. This is the revised version of the author's London University PhD dissertation.

108 **The foundation of Dutch power in Ceylon (1638-1658).**
Karunadasa Wijesiri Goonewardena.   Amsterdam: Djambatan, 1958. 196p. 3 maps. bibliog.

Focuses on the two decades leading up to the successful establishment of Dutch rule over the littoral of Sri Lanka. The work is particularly valuable for its account of Dutch relations with the principal indigenous ruler, Rājasimha II, with whom they concluded a treaty in 1638. This treaty provided the basis for their intervention in the Sinhalese king's struggle against the Portuguese. This is the published version of the author's London University doctoral dissertation.

109 **Dutch historical writing on South Asia.**
Karunadasa Wijesiri Goonewardena.   In: *Historians of India, Pakistan and Ceylon*. Edited by C. H. Philips.   London: Oxford University Press, 1961, p. 170-82.

A critical review of Dutch sources for the study of the Dutch East India Company's rule over the littoral of Sri Lanka between 1658 and 1796.

110 **Agrarian policies of the Dutch in South-West Ceylon, 1743-1767.**
Don Ariyapala Kotelawele.   *Afdeling Agrarische Geschiedenis Bijdragen*, vol. 14 (1967), p. 3-33.

The Dutch East India Company's policies of monopolistic trade, its attitude towards the expansion of subsistence agriculture, and its efforts to regularize land revenue by the compilation of land registers (*thombo*) are discussed in this important essay. The author's conclusion considers the strains which these several policies imposed upon the Sinhalese social order of the early 18th century.

31

111   **Ceylon: the Portuguese era being a history of the island for the period 1505-1658.**
Paul Edward Pieris.   Colombo: Colombo Apothecaries, 1913-14. 2 vols.

The first modern scholarly study to be based on historical sources both in Sri Lanka and Portugal, this remains the only general work in English on Portuguese rule in Sri Lanka. More specialized recent work has made parts of this study outdated.

112   **Ceylon and the Hollanders, 1658-1796.**
Paul Edward Pieris.   Colombo: Colombo Apothecaries, 1947. 3rd ed. 122p. bibliog.

A pioneering survey of Dutch rule over the littoral of Sri Lanka, this work can still be consulted for the main political developments of the period.

113   **Sinhalese social organization: the Kandyan period.**
Ralph Pieris.   Colombo: Ceylon University Press Board, 1956. 311p. map.

Kandyan social structure, the village organization, social stratification, kinship and marriage are emphasised in this study, but the author also considers the political organization of the Kandyan Kingdom. Impressive for the richness of the data presented, this is the standard work on the Kandyan society and polity as they stood at the time of the British conquest of Kandy in 1815.

114   **The temporal and spiritual conquest of Ceylon.**
Fernao de Queyroz, translated by Simon Gregory Perera.   New York: AMS Press, 1975. 2 vols.

This monumental work by a Jesuit missionary, written in 1687 in the form of six books, covers Portuguese rule in Sri Lanka. It is the most important historical source for the study of Portuguese rule, and historians have placed a high value on its refreshing candour. This translation first appeared in 1930.

115   **The historic tragedy of the island of Ceilao, dedicated to His Most Serene Majesty Dom Pedro the Second, King of Portugal, Our Lord.**
João Ribeiro, translated from the Portuguese by Paulus Edward Pieris.   Colombo: Ceylon Daily News Press, 1948. 4th ed. 266p.

Although first published in Lisbon in 1836, this work was completed in 1685. Ribeiro, who lived in southwest Sri Lanka for eighteen years, writes from the perspective of a common Portuguese soldier. His descriptions of both the Portuguese and the local population and the events that took place provide valuable information to the historian of Portuguese Sri Lanka.

116   **Francois Valentijn's description of Ceylon.**
François Valentijn, edited and translated by Sinnappah
Arasaratnam. London: Hakluyt Society, 1978. 395p. 7 maps.
bibliog. (Hakluyt Society, series 2, vol. 149).

Drawn from Valentijn's five-volume *Oud en nieuw Oost-Indien*, published in
Amsterdam in 1724-26, this work presents the first twelve chapters of Valentijn's
description of Sri Lanka, its history up to the expulsion of the Portuguese by the
Dutch in 1658, and its geography, society and institutions. Valentijn had no
personal experience of society in Sri Lanka and his biases and prejudices are
patent. Nonetheless, his description is remarkably sensitive as well as vivid, and it
stands as one of the most important historical sources for the early colonial
period.

117   **The fatal history of Portuguese Ceylon: transition to Dutch rule.**
George Davison Winius. Cambridge, Massachusetts: Harvard
University Press, 1971. 215p. 3 maps. bibliog.

The last phase of Portuguese rule in maritime Sri Lanka, the years 1594 to 1658,
is examined in this study which was originally submitted as a PhD thesis to
Columbia University. Developments in Sri Lanka are intertwined with those in
Goa and Europe, with particular attention devoted to Portuguese-Dutch
relations. The author concludes that the Portuguese effectively abandoned Sri
Lanka to the Dutch with the shift in their interest from the Indian Ocean to South
America.

An historical relation of Ceylon . . .
See item no. 6.

Religion and legitimation of power in Sri Lanka.
See item no. 216.

Collective identities, nationalisms and protest in modern Sri Lanka.
See item no. 300.

**A sketch of the constitution of the Kandyan Kingdom and other relevant
papers.**
See item no. 329.

The legal system of Ceylon in its historical setting.
See item no. 337.

**The history of Ceylon (c.1500-1658): a historiographical and biblio-
graphical survey.**
See item no. 620.

British rule (1796-1948)

118 **The administration of Sir Henry Ward. Governor of Ceylon, 1855-1860.**
S. V. Balasingham. Dehiwala, Sri Lanka: Tisara Prakasakayo, 1968. 142p. bibliog. (Ceylon Historical Journal, vol. 11).
Studies the tenure of one of the most assertive and successful British governors of the 19th century, and discusses in detail Ward's policies on coffee, transportation, immigration of Indian labour for the coffee plantations, irrigation and agriculture, and social welfare. This is the published version of the author's London University master's dissertation.

119 **The handbook of the Ceylon National Congress 1919-1928.**
Edited by Soloman West Ridgeway Dias Bandaranaike.
Colombo: H. W. Cave, 1928. 912p.
A collection of documents of the Ceylon National Congress, the major political organization which was active during a crucial stage in the evolution of the nationalist movement in Sri Lanka.

120 **The administration of Sir William Gregory. Governor of Ceylon 1872-1877.**
Bertram Bastiampillai. Dehiwala, Sri Lanka: Tisara Prakasakayo, 1968. 188p. bibliog. (Ceylon Historical Journal, vol. 12).
An examination of the policies of a governor who is characterized by the author as one of the outstanding 'pro-consuls' of the 19th century. Gregory's policies towards the plantation industry, transportation, social reform, rural development, education, and administrative machinery are detailed. This is the published version of the author's London University master's dissertation.

121 **Ceylon and its capabilities, an account of its natural resources, indigenous productions, and commercial facilities, to which are added details of its statistics, piloting and sailing directions, and an appendix containing the Royal Charter of Justice, the Kandyan Convention of 1815, Ordinances of the Colonial Government on various matters connected with the commerce of that island, etc.**
John Whitchurch Bennett. London: William H. Allen, 1843. 427p. map.
The work of yet another British civil servant, this was written with the goal of publicising the value of the colony to England. Its coverage is comprehensive, and it is an important source for the study of the first fifty years of British rule.

122   A view of the agricultural, commercial and financial interests of
      Ceylon with an appendix containing some of the principal laws and
      usages of the Candians; port and custom-house regulations, tables
      of exports and imports, public revenue and expenditures, etc.
      Anthony Bertolacci.   London: Black, Parbury & Allen, 1817.
      577p. map.

The work of a civil servant who served in Sri Lanka from 1798 to 1814, this is one
of the most valuable sources for the study of the early period of British rule.

123   The Royal Navy and Trincomalee. The history of their connection,
      c.1750-1958.
      H. A. Colgate.   *Ceylon Journal of Historical and Social Studies*,
      vol. 7, no. 1 (Jan.-June 1964), p. 1-16.

Highlights the strategic importance of the port of Trincomalee for the Royal Navy
over a period of two hundred years.

124   Public administration in Ceylon.
      Charles Henry Collins.   London: Oxford University Press for the
      Royal Institute of International Affairs, 1951. 162p. bibliog.

A survey of the developments in public administration during the period of
British rule.

125   A description of Ceylon, containing an account of the country,
      inhabitants and natural productions; with narratives of a tour
      round the island in 1800, the campaign in Candy in 1803, and a
      journey to Ramisseram in 1804.
      James Cordiner.   London: Longman, Hurst, Rees & Orme;
      Aberdeen, Scotland: A. Brown, 1807. 2 vols.

The first major English publication on Sri Lanka after the British conquest of its
maritime provinces, this, in many respects, set the tone for the numerous other
works which were to appear in the following decades of the 19th century. The
author was the chaplain to the Garrison at Colombo from 1799 to 1804, and was a
close confidant of the first British governor, Sir Fredrick North.

126   Ceylon at the census of 1911, being a review of the results of the
      census of 1911.
      Edward Brandis Denham.   Colombo: Government Printer, 1912.
      538p. maps.

Now recognized as a classic, this superb analysis of the census data of 1911 is a
mine of information on social and economic developments under the British and
it has proved exceedingly valuable to the researcher.

127 **Ceylon under the British occupation, 1795-1832: its political, administrative and economic development.**
Colvin Reginald de Silva.   Colombo: Colombo Apothecaries, 1962. 4th ed. 2 vols.
This study, first published in 1941-42, remains the most detailed treatment of the first phase of British rule in Sri Lanka. The first volume is devoted to political history and the development of the administrative structure, and the second to the economy.

128 **Social policy and missionary organizations in Ceylon, 1840-1855.**
Kingsley Muthumuni de Silva.   London: Longmans for the Royal Commonwealth Society, 1965. 318p. bibliog.
A study of the role played by the Christian missionary organizations in the shaping of the religious and social policy of the British in mid-19th-century Sri Lanka. The first part of the study examines the successful agitation conducted by the organizations to sever the connection between the state and Buddhism, established when the Kandyan Kingdom was ceded to the British in 1815. The second part discusses the evolution of education policy and missionary concerns with caste, slavery and the Veddas. The final part deals with missionary activities in relation to the immigration of South Indian labour to the plantations. A revised version of the author's London University doctoral thesis, this is the first major scholarly study to focus on the social policy of the British in Sri Lanka.

129 **History of Ceylon from the beginning of the nineteenth century to 1948.**
Edited by Kingsley Muthumuni de Silva.   Colombo: University of Ceylon, Peradeniya, 1973. 579p. 6 maps. bibliog. (University of Ceylon History of Ceylon, vol. 3).
Written by Sri Lankan historians, who offer syntheses of the specialist literature as well as original research in their respective essays, this is the most comprehensive treatment of British rule available in a single volume. Part one examines the initial phase of British rule up to 1833. Part two focuses on the consolidation of British power and the social and economic changes that took place in the following decades of the 19th century. Themes such as élite formation, demography, transportation, judiciary and literature, which cut across the broad periodization followed, are discussed in part three. The final part covers the 20th century and includes discussions on the constitutional changes, bureaucracy, economy, land and social policies and the transfer of power. A full bibliography is included.

130 **A history of the Ceylon police, vol. II. (1866-1913).**
A. C. Dep.   Colombo: Times of Ceylon, 1969. 527p. bibliog.
The development of the police force from the reforms of the 1860s to 1913 is examined in this work. The author's concern is with the institutional aspects.

131   **Forty years of official and unofficial life in an oriental crown colony, being the life of Sir Richard F. Morgan, Kt., Queen's Advocate and acting Chief Justice of Ceylon.**
William Digby.   Madras, India: Higginbotham, 1879. 2 vols.

This biography of Sir Richard Morgan, the distinguished Burgher lawyer who was a dominant figure in the public life of the colony in the second half of the 19th century, is rich in detail and marvellously evokes the political and social milieu of the period. This is a valuable historical source for the study of British rule.

132   **A hundred years of Ceylonese in Malaysia and Singapore (1867-1967), being records and recollections of a community.**
Sabathipillai Durai Raja Singham.   Kuala Lumpur: the author, 1968. 433p.

This compilation offers anecdotal information about the history of the Sri Lankan Tamils in the two countries. The principal attraction for the Tamils, that of openings in the lower echelons of the bureaucracy of the British, is made evident.

133   **Eleven years in Ceylon, comprising sketches of the field sports and natural history of that colony, and an account of its history and antiquities.**
Jonathan Forbes.   Farnborough, England: Gregg International, 1972. 779p.

The memoir of the author's service as a military officer and as a civil servant in the interior of Sri Lanka, this was first published in two volumes in 1840 in London by Richard Bentley. Forbes' descriptions of the island and its people are carefully drawn, and he effectively communicates his enthusiasm for the 'noble sport' of elephant shooting and for archaeology.

134   **British governors of Ceylon.**
Herbert Alexander Jayatilleke Hulugalle.   Colombo: Associated Newspapers of Ceylon, 1963. 252p. bibliog.

This book presents biographical data on and the notable achievements of the British governors of Sri Lanka from 1798 to 1948.

135   **Ceylon: the path to independence.**
Charles Jeffries.   London: Pall Mall Press, 1962. 148p. map.

An account of the negotiations for transfer of power between the Sri Lankan leaders and the British by a Colonial Office official who was associated with the negotiations.

136   **The history of the Ceylon civil service, 1802-1833.**
P. D. Kannangara.   Dehiwala, Sri Lanka: Tisara Prakasakayo,
1966. 287p. bibliog. (Ceylon Historical Journal Monograph Series,
vol. 1).

A study, based on the author's London University doctoral dissertation, of the
formative years of the bureaucratic organization which was to play a central role
in the British colonial administration.

137   **A gazetteer of the Central Province of Ceylon.**
Archibald Campbell Lawrie.   Colombo: Government Printer,
1896, 1898. 2 vols.

The best known of the gazetteers published during British rule, this is a source of
rich and fascinating information about the places and people of the Central
Province. The Central Province encompassed the heart of the Kandyan Kingdom,
which was the last Sinhalese kingdom.

138   **The modern history of Ceylon.**
Evelyn Frederick Charles Ludowyk.   London: Weidenfeld &
Nicolson; New York, Washington, DC: Praeger, 1966. 308p.
2 maps. bibliog. (Asia-Africa Series of Modern Histories; Praeger
Asia-Africa Series).

A detailed treatment of British rule, along with a survey of the developments
since independence. The author's underlying argument is that the basic economic
structure, which was established with the rise of the coffee industry in the 1830s
and which remained unchanged during British rule, provides the clue to the
understanding of Sri Lanka's history.

139   **Buddhism in Sinhalese society, 1750-1900: a study of religious
revival and change.**
Kitsiri Malalgoda.   Berkeley, California; Los Angeles; London:
University of California Press, 1976. 300p. map. bibliog.

Two major themes are explored in this study: the schisms within the Buddhist
order and the rise of new monastic fraternities in the period up to 1865; and the
Buddhist-Christian confrontation in the later 19th century, which resulted in the
emergence of what is identified as Protestant Buddhism. The argument that the
strength derived from the internal organizational changes in the earlier period
enabled the Buddhists to withstand and respond with vigour to Christianity forms
the connecting link between the two themes.

140   **Ceylon under the British.**
Garrett Champness Mendis.   Colombo: Colombo Apothecaries,
1948. rev. ed. 138p. 10 maps. bibliog.

This survey of British rule, despite its age, can still be usefully consulted for major
historical developments of the 19th and 20th centuries.

141 **The Colebrooke-Cameron papers. Documents on British colonial policy in Ceylon, 1796-1833.**
Edited by Garrett Champness Mendis. Oxford: Oxford University Press, 1956. 2 vols.

These two volumes bring together the most important official documents relating to the first phase of British rule in Sri Lanka. Included are the charters of justice, the Kandyan Convention of 1815 which ceded the Kingdom of Kandy to the British, and the reports of the Colebrooke-Cameron commission of inquiry which made a wide-ranging and detailed investigation of the colonial government and conditions in the colony between 1829 and 1831. The editor's lengthy introduction discusses the evolution of colonial policy towards Sri Lanka during the period and the significance of the reports of the Colebrooke-Cameron commission, whose recommendations led to major reforms in colonial governance in 1833.

142 **The advent of the British to Ceylon, 1762-1803.**
Vernon Lorraine Benjamin Mendis. Dehiwala, Sri Lanka: Tisara Prakasakayo, 1971. 226p. bibliog.

Discusses the early information gathering diplomatic missions of the English East India Company to the King of Kandy, the emergence of a conscious policy to establish commercial and territorial interests, the supplanting of the Dutch who ruled the maritime regions in 1796, and the declaration of the Maritime Provinces as a crown colony in 1802 which ended the rule of the East India Company. The importance of events in Europe for developments in Sri Lanka are emphasized. This study is based on the author's London University MA thesis.

143 **Ceylon under British rule, 1795-1932, with an account of the East India Company's embassies to Kandy, 1762-1795.**
Lennox Algernon Mills. London: Cass, 1964. 312p. bibliog.

First published in 1932, this was one of the first studies to document British rule in Sri Lanka on the basis of the Colonial Office records. In many respects, this work has been superseded by later writings but it still can be consulted with profit.

144 **1915 Riots in Ceylon: a symposium.**
Journal of Asian Studies, vol. 29, no. 2 (Feb. 1970), p. 219-66.

This symposium focuses on the first major ethnic conflict in modern Sri Lanka, the Sinhalese-Muslim conflict which is identified in the historiography as the 1915 Riots. The causes of the riots, the British response, and the post-riots campaign for justice, which was the first occasion where agitational techniques were deployed by the emerging nationalist leaders, are examined.

145 **Tri-Sinhala: the last phase 1796-1815.**
Paul Edward Pieris. Colombo: Colombo Apothecaries, 1939. 248p. bibliog.

This study, by a historian avowedly presenting the nationalist perspective, provides a detailed examination of Kandyan-British relations up to the end of the Kandyan Kingdom.

146 **Sinhalē and the patriots, 1815-1818.**
Paul Edward Pieris. Colombo: Colombo Apothecaries, 1950.
742p. bibliog.

A graphic account of the early years of British rule in the Kandyan Provinces and the Rebellion of 1818, which was the first major open resistance to the British in the territory.

147 **A history of the Ceylon police, vol. I. 1795-1870.**
G. K. Pippet. Colombo: Times of Ceylon, 1938. 372p. map.

The pioneering study on the police, this examines the development of the police force under the British from its beginnings to the major reforms which were introduced in the 1860s.

148 **The Kandyan wars: the British army in Ceylon, 1803-18.**
Geoffrey Powell. London: Leo Cooper, 1977. 2nd ed. 320p.
2 maps. bibliog. (19th Century Military Campaigns).

A military historian's detailed account of the successive military campaigns which the British conducted against the Kandyan king until the kingdom was finally subjugated in 1815. The British army's harsh but successful efforts to put down the Rebellion of the Kandyans in 1818 are also recounted. The study offers a fascinating picture of how a conventional army eventually adapted itself to the guerilla warfare of the Kandyans.

149 **Indian estate labour in Ceylon during the coffee period (1830-1880).**
Michael Roberts. *Indian Economic and Social History Review*,
vol. 3, no. 1 (March 1966), p. 1-52; vol. 3, no. 2 (June 1966),
p. 101-36.

Examines the immigration of Indian Tamil labour to the Sri Lankan plantations, with attention devoted to both 'push and pull' factors, the marginal living conditions in South India and the relatively attractive conditions which existed in the plantations. The recruitment methods and structural changes in the migration – from a seasonal pattern at the beginning to longer-term settlement by the end of the period – are also discussed.

150 **Documents of the Ceylon National Congress and nationalist politics in Ceylon, 1929-1950.**
Edited by Michael Roberts. Colombo: Department of National Archives, 1977. 4 vols.

A comprehensive collection of documents relating to the working of the Ceylon National Congress, the organization which provided the political baptism for a generation of nationalist leaders. The editor's introduction entitled 'Elites, nationalisms, and the nationalist movement in British Ceylon' is worthy of special notice.

151 **Elite conflict in Sri Lanka and Sinhalese perspectives: barriers to accommodation.**
Michael Roberts. *Modern Asian Studies*, vol. 12, no. 3 (July 1978), p. 353-76.

The author discusses the failure of the Sinhalese élite, who dominated the Ceylon National Congress, the premier nationalist organization of the 1920s and 1930s, to work towards more accommodating policies, and the consequent emergence of Sinhalese-Tamil ethnic tension in the early 1920s. The article considers the reasons for this failure and the dilemma the Sinhalese leadership faced – in what circumstances do concessions placate sectional interests and what guarantee is there that further demands would not be stimulated by the concessions?

152 **British justice and the 'Oriental peasantry': the working of the colonial legal system in nineteenth century Sri Lanka.**
Vijaya Samaraweera. In: *British imperial policy in India and Sri Lanka 1815-1912: a reassessment.* Edited by N. Gerald Barrier, Robert I. Crane. New Delhi: Heritage Publishers; Columbia, Missouri: South Asia Books, 1981, p. 107-41.

This essay focuses on how the British officials conceptualized the role of the legal system they imposed on Sri Lanka in the 19th century. It examines the working of the legal system and points out that it failed to achieve the goals projected for it and that this failure was manifested in two crucial ways, in the distortion of its structural arrangements and in the emergence of the phenomenon of litigation.

153 **Fifty years in Ceylon. An autobiography.**
Thomas Skinner, edited by Annie Skinner. Dehiwala, Sri Lanka: Tisara Prakasakayo, 1974. 224p.

For forty years, beginning in 1818, the author was in charge of opening up Sri Lanka and this autobiography primarily deals with his road building work. However, in recounting his experiences, Skinner writes with perception and insight about the country and its people. His admiration for the classical civilizations sets him apart from the other writers of the 19th century. This is a reprint of the original edition published in London in 1891 by W. H. Allen.

154 **Diaries in Ceylon 1908-1911. Records of a colonial administrator, being the official diaries maintained by Leonard Woolf while Assistant Government Agent of the Hambantota District, Ceylon, during the period August 1908 to May 1911.**
Edited with a preface by Leonard Woolf. London: Hogarth Press, 1963. new ed. 286p.

These official diaries provide a valuable picture of the working of the district administration of the British in the early 20th century. They also illustrate the attitude and thinking of Woolf towards the people he was ruling as well as towards the imperial raj he embodied in his person as the district administrator. The original edition was published in Dehiwala, Sri Lanka, by the Ceylon Historical Journal.

Twentieth century impressions of Ceylon; its history, people, commerce, industries and resources.
See item no. 14.

Managing ethnic tensions in multi-ethnic societies: Sri Lanka 1880-1985.
See item no. 274.

A statistical survey of elections to the legislatures of Sri Lanka, 1911-1977.
See item no. 285.

Universal franchise, 1931-1981: the Sri Lankan experience.
See item no. 286.

Collective identities, nationalisms and protest in modern Sri Lanka
See item no. 300.

Civil service administration in Ceylon. A study in bureaucratic adaptation.
See item no. 321.

Notes on the constitutional law of colonial Ceylon.
See item no. 332.

The legal system of Ceylon in its historical setting.
See item no. 337.

The legislatures of Ceylon, 1928-1948.
See item no. 338.

The institutes of the laws of Ceylon.
See item no. 343.

Government and politics in Ceylon, 1931-1946.
See item no. 346.

Economic opinion and policy in Ceylon.
See item no. 366.

Ceylon: an export economy in transition.
See item no. 369.

Land tenure in village Ceylon: a sociological and historical study.
See item no. 413.

The rise of the labor movement in Ceylon.
See item no. 449.

Independent Sri Lanka (1948-.)

155 Insurgency 1971. An account of the April insurrection in Sri Lanka.
Anthony Christopher Alles. Colombo: Colombo Apothecaries, 1977. 2nd ed. 7 maps. bibliog.
A useful detailed account of the April 1971 Insurrection by the Marxist People's Liberation Front, or Janatha Vimukti Peramuna (JVP). The author, a Judge of the Supreme Court of Sri Lanka, was a member of the Criminal Justice Commission set up to try the offences arising out of the insurrection.

156 Explosion in a subcontinent: India, Pakistan, Bangladesh and Ceylon.
Edited by Robin Blackburn. Harmondsworth, England: Penguin, 1975. 379p. map.
The two contributions on Sri Lanka in this volume focus on the 1971 insurgency of the Janatha Vimukti Peramuna (JVP). Given his Marxist theoretical approach, Fred Halliday's interpretation of the insurgency is predictable but his essay offers an excellent, succinct account of the events that took place. The second contribution presents the speech of the leader of the JVP, Rohana Wijeweera, at his trial. A personal defence as well as a defence of the JVP, this is an invaluable source for understanding the revolutionary commitment of the JVP and its leader.

157 The people's rights; documents of the Civil Rights Movement of Sri Lanka, 1971 to 1978.
Civil Rights Movement of Sri Lanka. Colombo: Samanala, 1979. 149p.
An invaluable collection of documents pertaining to the issues in which the Civil Rights Movement was involved. It provides ample testimony to the serious inroads the state made on the civil rights and liberties of Sri Lankans in the 1970s.

158 Sri Lanka since independence.
Edited by Kingsley Muthumuni de Silva, Alfred Jeyaratnam Wilson, Calvin A. Woodward, W. Howard Wriggins. *Ceylon Journal of Historical and Social Studies*, new series, vol. 4, nos. 1-2 (1974), p. 1-157.
This collection focuses on events in Sri Lanka from 1948 to 1974. The emphasis is on political developments, with essays on the transfer of power, leadership perspectives, parliamentary government, bureaucracy, foreign policy, nationalism, the party system, Marxists and problems of communalism. Economic developments are reviewed in two articles. The studies of religion examine the interaction of religion and politics, the role of Christians in a Buddhist majority polity, and Buddhism, Hinduism and Islam.

159 **Coup theories and officers' motives: Sri Lanka in comparative perspective.**
Donald L. Horowitz. Princeton, New Jersey: Princeton University Press, 1980. 239p.

This study is concerned with understanding the motivations of the military and police officers who participated in the abortive coup against the government of Sirimavo Bandaranaike in 1962. The event is placed within the context of the changes which took place in the preceding six years, and the attempted coup is categorized as a 'reconstructive coup' or in other words, as an attempt to purify a contaminated political system. A wealth of information about the coup participants is presented but several puzzles remain unanswered, of which the most important is what precisely the officers sought to reconstitute through the coup.

160 **The Ceylon Insurrection of 1971.**
Robert N. Kearney, Janice Jiggins. *Journal of Commonwealth and Comparative Politics*, vol. 13, no. 1 (March 1975), p. 40-64.

A detailed examination of the April 1971 Insurrection, with a particularly useful discussion of the goals and recruitment methods of the Janatha Vimukti Peramuna.

161 **Sri Lanka in change and crisis.**
Edited by James Manor. New York: St Martin's Press, 1984. 229p. map. bibliog.

This book consists of two parts. The five contributions to part one consider the implications of two important political events of late 1982: the presidential election and the referendum, which called for a popular vote on the Jayewardene government's decision to extend the life of Parliament. Part two deals with the racial violence of July and August 1983. Several of the six contributors to this part offer descriptions of the violence, with some attempts at explanations. The most valuable contribution is Gananath Obeyesekere's penetrating discussion of the institutionalization of political violence, in particular since 1977. The editor's introduction discusses the developments which took place since the Jayewardene government came to power in 1977.

162 **Some comments on the social backgrounds of the April 1971 insurgency in Sri Lanka (Ceylon).**
Gananath Obeyesekere. *Journal of Asian Studies*, vol. 33, no. 3 (May 1974), p. 367-83.

Using unpublished, officially compiled data on 10,192 suspected 'insurgents', the author examines the caste, educational and occupational backgrounds of those involved in the April 1971 Insurrection, and considers the implications of the data for the élite-dominated politics of post-independence Sri Lanka.

163 **The revolt in the temple composed to commemorate 2500 years of the land, the race and the faith.**

D. C. Vijayavardhana. Colombo: Sinha Publishers, 1953. 700p.

This polemical work, with its vivid articulation of the powerlessness of the Sinhalese Buddhists in the face of minority groups and the advocation of state intervention on behalf of Buddhism and Buddhists, exerted a powerful influence in the mid-1950s, and it is an important source for understanding the Sinhalese Buddhist populism of the period.

164 **Symposium on Sri Lanka.**

Edited by W. A. Wiswa Warnapala. *Asian Survey*, vol. 13, no. 12 (Dec. 1973), p. 1,121-92.

A collection of five essays, laudatory in tone, exploring policy changes in the areas of external relations, management of internal and external finances, development policy, education and constitutional reform undertaken by the United Front government which came into power in 1970, under Sirimavo Bandaranaike.

165 **Ceylon: dilemmas of a new nation.**

W. Howard Wriggins. Princeton, New Jersey: Princeton University Press, 1960. 505p. 8 maps. bibliog.

An important work on political developments in independent Sri Lanka. The volume examines, in turn, factors which shaped the setting of politics and three overriding themes in domestic politics: religious revivalism and cultural nationalism; the problem of national unity; and issues in economic development. The discussion of the themes in domestic politics is conducted within the context of the electoral triumph of S. W. R. D. Bandaranaike and this account is essential reading for the understanding of this crucial event in modern Sri Lankan history.

Sri Lanka: a survey.
See item no. 4.

Modern Sri Lanka: a society in transition.
See item no. 5.

Sri Lanka in transition.
See item no. 76.

Discrimination in Sri Lanka.
See item no. 273.

The states of South Asia: problems of national integration. Essays in honor of W. H. Morris-Jones.
See item no. 283.

Elite politics in the new states: the case of post-independent Sri Lanka.
See item no. 287.

Population
and Family Planning

166 **Fertility trends in Ceylon.**
O. E. R. Abhayaratne, C. H. S. Jayawardene. Colombo:
Colombo Apothecaries, 1967. 421p. maps. bibliog.

The authors analyse demographic data for the period 1900 to 1960 in part one of this study and in part two they report the results of village surveys undertaken in the mid-1960s.

167 **Family planning in Ceylon.**
O. E. R. Abhayaratne, C. H. S. Jayawardene. Colombo:
Colombo Apothecaries, 1968. 188p. bibliog.

This study provides a survey of population policy in Sri Lanka, the results of the sample survey conducted at two suburban family planning clinics, and a discussion of the effectiveness of the family planning promotion campaigns in the suburbs of Colombo.

168 **Population, land and structural change in Sri Lanka and Thailand.**
Edited by James Brow. *Contributions to Asian Studies*, vol. 9
(1976), p. 1-113.

Includes three papers on Sri Lanka: land use and population growth in colonial Sri Lanka by Patrick Peebles; the impact of population growth on the agricultural practices and settlement patterns of the Anuradhapura Veddas by James Brow; and kinship and land rights in the context of demographic change by Anthony Joseph Selvadurai.

169 **Population problems of Sri Lanka.**
Demographic Training and Research Unit, University of Sri
Lanka, Colombo Campus.   Colombo: Demographic Training and
Research Unit, 1976. 265p. 5 maps. bibliog.

A collection of essays by specialists in their respective fields covering the themes
of the growth and distribution of population, fertility and family planning,
migration and urbanization, and population policy. The coverage is comprehensive but the volume suffers from the uneven quality of the essays included.

170 **Comparative study of population growth and agricultural change.
Case study of Sri Lanka.**
Economic and Social Commission for Asia and the Pacific.
Bangkok: United Nations, 1975. 112p. bibliog. (Asian Population
Studies Series, no. 23).

The theme of this case-study, which covers the period 1946 to 1971, is the
interrelationship between demographic factors and agricultural change. Population changes, internal migration, agricultural changes, the relationship between
agricultural and demographic changes, and sociological features pertinent to the
theme receive attention.

171 **Population of Sri Lanka.**
Economic and Social Commission for Asia and the Pacific.
Bangkok: United Nations, 1976. 397p. 2 maps.

Population trends, past, current and future, and their implications for social
welfare measures and for demographic changes are examined in detail in this
valuable study.

172 **Urbanization in Ceylon, 1946-63.**
Gavin W. Jones, S. Selvaratnam.   *Modern Ceylon Studies*, vol. 1,
no. 2 (July 1970), p. 199-212.

A review of the process of urbanization between 1946 and 1963 on the basis of
census data. The authors note that the growth in the urban population was only
marginally faster than the rural population and that the rural/urban dichotomy is
markedly less sharp in Sri Lanka than in many countries of Asia.

173 **Family planning in Ceylon.**
Shelton Upatissa Kodikara.   In: *The politics of family planning.*
Edited by T. Edward Smith. London: Allen & Unwin, 1973,
p. 291-334.

A survey of family planning in Sri Lanka beginning with the establishment of the
Family Planning Association in 1953.

174 **Malaria eradication and its effect on mortality levels: a discussion.**
Peter Newman, Sirimewan Ananda Meegama. *Population Studies*, vol. 23, no. 2 (July 1969), p. 285-306.

An exchange of views by two scholars who have investigated an important issue in Sri Lanka's demographic history, the role of the malaria eradication campaign in the declining mortality rates of the post-Second World War period.

175 **The demography of Ceylon.**
N. K. Sarkar. Colombo: Government Press, 1957. 288p. 2 maps.

The first major monograph on the demography of Sri Lanka, this work examines the history of population, trends in marriage, fertility and mortality, and the socioeconomic factors which had an impact upon demographic changes. Data up to 1950 is covered.

176 **World fertility survey: Sri Lanka 1975.**
Sri Lanka. Department of Census and Statistics. Colombo: Department of Census and Statistics, 1978. 713p. map.

This report provides, on the basis of a national sample, a comprehensive analysis of fertility and contraceptive behaviour of Sri Lankans, with particular attention devoted to the decline in the birth rate recorded in the 1970s.

Sri Lanka: a survey.
See item no. 4.

Modern Sri Lanka: a society in transition.
See item no. 5.

Ceylon at the census of 1911, being a review of the results of the census of 1911.
See item no. 126.

History of Ceylon from the beginning of the nineteenth century to 1948.
See item no. 129.

Population growth and economic development in Ceylon.
See item no. 362.

Economic implications of population growth. Sri Lanka labour force, 1946-1981.
See item no. 372.

Languages

General

177 A colloquial Sinhalese reader.
M. W. Sugathapala de Silva.   Heslington, York, England:
University of York Printing Unit, 1971. 211p.
A reader designed as a companion to *Colloquial Sinhalese* (q.v.).

178 Convergence in diglossia: the Sinhalese situation.
M. W. Sugathapala de Silva.   *International Journal of Dravidian
Linguistics*, vol. 3, no. 1 (Jan. 1974), p. 60-91.
An examination of the manner in which colloquial and literary Sinhalese converge
and the ways in which literary Sinhalese changes as a consequence.

179 Sinhalese and other island languages in South Asia.
M. W. Sugathapala de Silva.   Tübingen, GFR: Günter Narr
Verlag, 1979. 75p. bibliog. (Ars Linguistica 3).
A review of Sinhalese and Tamil linguistic studies by the best known Sri Lankan
linguist. The emphasis is on Sinhalese. An extensive bibliography, covering both
published works and unpublished dissertations, is provided.

**180 Nativism, diglossia and the Sinhalese identity in the language
problem in Sri Lanka.**
K. N. O. Dharmadasa.   *International Journal of the Sociology of
Language*, vol. 13 (1977), p. 21-32.
The paper deals with an important controversy which took place among the
Sinhalese speakers, regarding the choice of a written standard for their language.

The controversy centred around a group of 'purists' who looked towards the classical linguistic heritage for the standard. The author discusses the controversy within the colonial setting as well as within the context of the tensions that arose between the Sinhalese and Tamils in independent Sri Lanka.

181 **National languages of Sri Lanka – I. Sinhala.**
J. B. Dissanayaka. Colombo: Department of Cultural Affairs, 1976. 44p. (The Culture of Sri Lanka, no. 10).
A succinct survey of the Sinhalese language and its use.

182 **Linguistics in South Asia.**
Edited by Murray B. Emeneau, Charles A. Ferguson. The Hague, Paris: Mouton, 1969. 814p. (Current Trends in Linguistics, vol. 5).
Includes three papers which focus on Sri Lanka: M. W. S. de Silva on Sinhalese; D. E. Hettiarachchi on linguistics in general; and A. Sathasivam on Tamil linguistics. They each discuss the nature of the scholarship in their respective fields.

183 **Colloquial Sinhalese.**
Gordon H. Fairbanks, James Wells Gair, M. W. Sugathapala de Silva. Ithaca, New York: South Asia Program, Cornell University, 1968. 2 pts.
The basis of this pedagogic work is that colloquial Sinhalese deserves study in its own right. Intended for the beginner, the volumes contain thirty-six lessons.

184 **English and Sinhalese bilingualism.**
Chitra Fernando. *Language in Society*, vol. 6, no. 3 (Dec. 1977), p. 341-60.
A study of factors governing the language choice of Sinhalese bilinguals and the correlation of these factors with domains and role relations.

185 **Colloquial Sinhalese clause structures.**
James Wells Gair. The Hague: Mouton, 1970. 164p. bibliog. (Janua Linguarum, Series Practice, 83).
A significant study of Sinhalese clause types within a 'syntactic structure' model.

186 **Literary Sinhalese.**
James Wells Gair, W. S. Karunatilaka, with the assistance of Gregory Pearson, Heloise Perera. Ithaca, New York: South Asia Program and Department of Modern Languages and Linguistics, Cornell University, 1974. 429p.
An introductory text containing fifteen lessons.

187 **A grammar of the Sinhalese language.**
Wilhelm Geiger. Colombo: Royal Asiatic Society (Ceylon Branch), 1938. 200p.

This study represents the culmination of the work on the history and structure of the Sinhalese language carried out by the distinguished scholar.

188 **National languages of Sri Lanka – II. Tamil.**
K. Kailasapathy, A. Sanmugadas. Colombo: Department of Cultural Affairs, 1976. 33p. (The Culture of Sri Lanka, no. 11).

Tamil language and its use in Sri Lanka is succinctly surveyed.

189 **The Jaffna dialect of Tamil: a phonological study.**
Kandasamy Kanapathipillai. *Indian Linguistics*, vol. 19 (1958), p. 219-27.

An analysis of Tamil of Northern Sri Lanka as a dialect of the Tamil language of South India.

190 **A standard language and socio-historical parameters: standard Sri Lankan Tamil.**
Tiru Kandiah *International Journal of the Sociology of Language*, vol. 16 (1978), p. 59-76.

This article explores the emergence of standard Sri Lankan Tamil through the efforts of the Tamil élite who saw language as the means of unifying the Tamil-speaking population in their political struggle against the dominant Sinhalese élite.

191 **Phonology of Sinhalese and Sri Lankan Tamil. A study in contrast and interference.**
W. S. Karunatilaka, S. Suseendirarajah. *Indian Linguistics*, vol. 34, no. 3 (Sept. 1973), p. 180-91.

The only available contrastive analysis of Sinhalese and Tamil.

192 **The use and abuse of English: common errors in Ceylon English.**
Hector Augustus Passe. Madras, India: Oxford University Press, 1955. 135p.

The pioneer study of the use of the English language by Sri Lankans.

193 **The Tamil diglossia situation in Sri Lanka.**
Sabaratnasinghe Thananjayarajasingham. *Ceylon Historical Journal*, vol. 25, nos. 1-4 (1978), p. 275-84.

A leading Tamil linguist's analysis of the two principal varieties of Tamil spoken in Sri Lanka, their respective specialized functions, and the impact of the nativistic movement since 1948 on language use patterns.

194 **History of the Sinhalese noun: a morphological study based on inscriptions.**
D. J. Wijayaratne. Peradeniya, Sri Lanka: University of Ceylon Press Board, 1956. 217p. bibliog.
An exhaustive and systematic examination of noun morphology.

195 **Some features of Ceylon Tamil.**
Kamil Zvelebil. *Indo-Iranian Journal*, vol. 9, no. 2 (1966), p. 113-38.
The distinctiveness of Sri Lankan Tamil is brought out in this paper.

Dictionaries

196 **An English-Sinhalese dictionary.**
Charles Carter. Colombo: M. D. Gunasena, 1965. 535p.
The standard work, first published in 1891. This reprint is of the revised edition of 1936.

197 **A Sinhalese-English dictionary.**
Charles Carter. Colombo: M. D. Gunasena, 1965. 806p.
First published in 1924, this work continues to be recognized as the best Sinhalese-English dictionary.

198 **A dictionary of the Sinhalese language.**
Colombo: Royal Asiatic Society (Ceylon Branch), 1935-1941, University of Ceylon, 1957-.
First mooted and undertaken by the Ceylon Branch of the Royal Asiatic Society (vol. 1, parts 1-6), and continued by the University of Ceylon (vol. 1, part 7), in both cases under the editorship of distinguished scholars, this ambitious project has faced several setbacks and it is not clear when it will be completed. That which has been published so far is valuable and authoritative.

199 **An etymological and comparative lexicon of the Tamil language, with indexes of words quoted in Indo-European languages.**
Saminder Gnanaprakasar. Chunnakam, Sri Lanka: Thirukamal Press, 1938-46. vol. I, pts. 1-6.
This lexicon, which was incomplete at the time of the author's death, is widely used, though its methodology has been criticised by later scholars.

200   **English-Sinhalese dictionary.**
      Gunapala Piyasena Malalasekera.   Colombo: M. D. Gunasena,
      1978. 1,066p.
First published in 1948 and subsequently revised several times, this is a widely
used dictionary.

201   **English-Pāli dictionary.**
      Ambalangoda Polvatte Buddhadatta.   London: Luzac for Pāli
      Text Society, 1970. 588p.
This authoritative dictionary was first published in 1955.

202   **Tamil lexicon.**
      University of Madras.   Madras, India: University of Madras,
      1924-39. 6 vols.
This is the most popular Tamil dictionary in Sri Lanka, though it should be noted
that it does not cover usages peculiar to the Tamil-speakers in Sri Lanka.

Religion

General

203 **Religiousness in Sri Lanka.**
Edited by John Ross Carter. Colombo: Marga Institute, 1979.
300p. bibliog.

A collection of essays by adherents of Buddhism, Hinduism, Christianity and Islam in which they explore the meaning of religiousness in terms of their personal selves as well as within the context of the religious communities to which they belong.

204 **Sociology and anthropology of religion in Sri Lanka.**
Edited by François Houtart. *Social Compass*, vol. 20, no. 2
(1973), p. 99-399.

The principal focus in this collection is on Buddhism. Three essays consider the practice of Buddhism at the popular level, and three others discuss respectively the Buddhist ordination rite, the role of Buddhist monks in the 1956 parliamentary elections and the work of the Buddhist philosopher, K. N. Jayatilleke. Historical dimensions are offered in the essays on the Buddhist-Christian confrontation in the 19th century and on the impact of westernizing and modernizing forces on Buddhism. The interrelationship of religion and politics among the Sinhalese is also examined, and the way Buddhists and Catholics view each other is the subject of another essay. The sole essay on Hinduism considers a popular religious cult. The text is in English and French (with abstracts in English).

205 **Religion and ideology in Sri Lanka.**
François Houtart. Colombo: Hansa Publishers, 1974. 541p. bibliog.

This study explores the relationship between religion and politics in Sri Lanka and documents the critical importance of the ideological function of religion in Sinhalese society, both in the past and in the contemporary setting. This is the published version of a doctoral dissertation submitted to the University of Louvain.

206 **The cult of goddess Pattini.**
Gananath Obeyesekere. Chicago; London: University of Chicago Press, 1984. 629p. bibliog.

This major work by the foremost interpreter of Sinhalese Buddhism is indispensable reading for the serious student of Sri Lanka. The core of the study is an ethnography of the cult of Pattini, a Hindu goddess who became an integral element in the Sinhalese Buddhist pantheon. This is more than a mere study of the Pattini cult. A wealth of data is offered on history, polity and society and the author's psychocultural analysis of the material results in fresh and at times provocative interpretation of religion and society in Sri Lanka.

207 **The Kataragama pilgrimage: Hindu-Buddhist interaction and its significance in Sri Lanka's polyethnic social system.**
Bryan Pfaffenberger. *Journal of Asian Studies*, vol. 38, no. 2 (Feb. 1979), p. 252-70.

This essay on the socioreligious phenomenon of Kataragama, a holy centre which attracts pilgrims from all the religious groups in Sri Lanka, concludes that while Kataragama appears on the surface to reflect Sinhalese Buddhist-Tamil Hindu cohesion and harmony, it in fact plays a central role in maintaining and enhancing ethnic hostilities and negative stereotypes held by the respective groups.

Sri Lanka: a survey.
See item no. 4.

Culture of Ceylon in mediaeval times.
See item no. 88.

Social policy and missionary organizations in Ceylon, 1840-1855.
See item no. 128.

History of Ceylon from the beginning of the nineteenth century to 1948.
See item no. 129.

Sri Lanka since independence.
See item no. 158.

Religion and politics in Sri Lanka.
See item no. 299.

Collective identities, nationalisms and protest in modern Sri Lanka.
See item no. 300.

Kataragama. The holiest place in Ceylon.
See item no. 541.

Buddhism

208 **The forest monks of Sri Lanka. An anthropological and historical study.**
Michael Carrithers. New Delhi: Oxford University Press, 1983.
306p. bibliog.

This study is concerned with forest monks, as opposed to those attached to village or urban temples, and examines, mainly through biographical data on individual monks, the way of life these monks sought to revive, the paths chosen by them, and the successes and failures they faced. This is a major contribution to the understanding of a vital phenomenon within Sinhalese Buddhism.

209 **Monks, priests and peasants. A study of Buddhism and social structure in central Ceylon.**
Hans-Dieter Evers. Leiden, the Netherlands: Brill, 1972. 136p. 5 maps. biblio. (Monographs in Social Anthropology and Theoretical Studies in Honour of Nels Anderson – 1).

The social, religious and economic organization of the Lankatilaka temple, the royal temple founded in 1344, is the subject of this study. The interrelationship between the different elements of the temple complex and the temple's relationship with the Kandyan state organization as well as the changes that took place in these relationships are also detailed.

210 **Precept and practice: traditional Buddhism in the rural highlands of Ceylon.**
Richard F. Gombrich. Oxford: Clarendon Press, 1979. 366p. bibliog.

Arguing that it is critically important to examine religious behaviour in relation to the textual traditions, this study offers the central thesis that Buddhism, as practised by the villagers studied, is doctrinally orthodox and that the structure of the beliefs and practices have remained essentially the same, though their content has undergone changes in some respects. This is the revised version of an Oxford University doctoral dissertation.

211 **Millennialism in relation to Buddhism.**
Kitsiri Malalgoda. *Comparative Studies in Society and History*,
vol. 12, no. 4 (Oct. 1970), p. 424-41.

The argument presented in this essay is that millennialism is not characteristically
a Judaeo-Christian phenomenon and that it can arise in other religious traditions as
well. The author offers the case of Sinhalese Buddhism and its concept of the
Sinhalese as the 'chosen people' which inspired millennial-style movements in
contexts of political subjugation and deprivation.

212 **The heritage of the bhikku: a short history of the bhikku in
educational, cultural, social and political life.**
Walpola Rahula, translated by K. P. G. Wijayasurendra, revised
by the author. New York: Grove, 1974. 176p. bibliog.

This extended essay, first published in 1946, is by a Buddhist monk who was
deeply involved in the controversy that arose in the 1940s over the role of
Buddhist monks in public affairs. The work is valuable for its perceptions of the
Buddhist monks who were to be increasingly attracted into political activism. A
postscript considers the developments since 1946.

213 **Rituals of the Kandyan state.**
H. L. Seneviratne. Cambridge, England: Cambridge University
Press, 1978. 190p. 6 maps. bibliog. (Cambridge Studies in Social
Anthropology, vol. 22).

An anthropologist's analysis of the Kandyan Sinhalese theory of society as a
balanced hierarchy that embraces both the social and natural orders, which was
made possible by the performance of rituals at the most important Buddhist
temple in Sri Lanka, the Temple of the Tooth at Kandy. There is an extended
discussion of the major ritual of the temple, the annual *perahara* or pageant. This
important study is the revised version of the author's doctoral dissertation
submitted to the University of Rochester.

214 **The two wheels of dhamma: essays on the Theravada tradition in
India and Ceylon.**
Edited by Bardwell L. Smith. Chambersburg, Pennsylvania:
American Academy of Religion, 1972. 121p. bibliog. (AAR
Studies in Religion, no. 3).

Essays on Sri Lanka include Bardwell L. Smith's discussion of the ideal social
order portrayed in the historical chronicles the *Mahāvaṃsa* and *Dīpavaṃsa*, and
his consideration of the problems of interpreting the capacity of Sinhalese
Buddhism to abet the process of modernization; Frank Reynolds's bibliographical
essay on Sinhalese Buddhism; and Gananath Obeyesekere's important study of
religious symbolism and political change, in which he examines changes in
Sinhalese Buddhism on the behavioural level and the political and social changes
which produced them.

215 **Tradition and change in Theravada Buddhism: essays on Ceylon and Thailand in the 19th and 20th centuries.**
Edited by Bardwell L. Smith. *Contributions to Asian Studies*, vol. 4 (1973).

Includes Heinz Bechert's essay on the contradictions in Sinhalese Buddhism, Balakrishna Govind Gokhale's examination of Anagarika Dharmapala, the central figure in the Buddhist revivalist movement, and P. T. M. Fernando's essay on the emergence of the English-educated élites in colonial times and their connection with Buddhist nationalism.

216 **Religion and legitimation of power in Sri Lanka.**
Edited by Bardwell L. Smith. Chambersburg, Pennsylvania: Anima Books, 1978. 244p. map. bibliog.

The question which is addressed by the majority of the contributors in this collection is, in what ways did Buddhism lend itself to the process of legitimation of power in Sri Lankan history? The question is considered in relation to the period of the classical civilizations in six essays which explore the themes of the relationship of the chronicles to the legitimation processes, myth and power in early history and Buddhist institutions in the legitimation processes. A bibliographical essay on the Polonnaruva period, which has little relevance to the issue of legitimation but which is nonetheless valuable, rounds up the focus on the classical civilizations. The legitimation role of Buddhism is taken up within the context of the Kandyan kingdom and in relation to the career of S. W. R. D. Bandaranaike in two other essays. Studies of the contradictions of Sinhalese Buddhism and the Sri Lanka Vinaya Vardana Society complete the collection.

217 **Buddhism in life. The anthropological study of religion and the Sinhalese practice of Buddhism.**
Martin Southwald. Manchester, England; Dover, New Hampshire: Manchester University Press, 1983. 232p. bibliog.

An anthropologist's account of Buddhism as it is thought and practised by village Sri Lanka.

Early history of Buddhism in Ceylon: or 'state of Buddhism in Ceylon as revealed by the Pali commentaries of the 5th century A.D.'
See item no. 84.

Robe and plough: monasticism and economic interest in early medieval Sri Lanka.
See item no. 91.

History of Buddhism in Ceylon. The Anurādhapura period, 3rd century BC-10th century AC.
See item no. 98.

Buddhism in Sinhalese society, 1750-1900: a study of religious revival and change.
See item no. 139.

Sri Lanka since independence.
See item no. 158.

Sociology and anthropology of religion in Sri Lanka.
See item no. 204.

Collective identities, nationalisms and protest in modern Sri Lanka.
See item no. 300.

Hinduism

218 **Hinduism in Ceylon.**
James Cartman. Colombo: M. D. Gunasena, 1957. 188p. 2 maps. bibliog.
This historical survey of Hinduism remains the only general work on the subject in the English language.

219 **Studies in Hinduism.**
Kandiah Navaratnam. Chunnakam, Sri Lanka: Thirumakal Press, 1973. 263p.
The published version of a lecture series on Hinduism and its study by non-Hindus delivered by the distinguished scholar of Tamil culture in Sri Lanka.

220 **The karmic theater. Self, society and astrology in Jaffna.**
Robert S. Perinbanayagam. Amherst, Massachusetts: University of Massachusetts Press, 1982. 212p. bibliog.
With the central focus on astrology, this study examines the interrelations of religion, astrology, self and society in Northern Sri Lanka. Though aimed at the specialist, this study could be consulted with profit by those who seek an understanding of the role of religion and popular religious practices within the Tamil community.

Sri Lanka: a survey.
See item no. 4

Sri Lanka since independence.
See item no. 158.

Caste in Tamil culture: the religious foundation of Sudra domination in Tamil Sri Lanka.
See item no. 235.

The laws and customs of the Tamils of Jaffna.
See item no. 340.

Christianity

221 **Opinions and attitudes of Catholics in Ceylon.**
François Houtart, Geneviève Lemercinier.   Louvain, Belgium: Centre de Recherches Socio-Religieuses, 1970. 2 vols.
A detailed and comprehensive attitudinal study of the Catholic community in Sri Lanka which is based on a survey carried out in 1969-70.

222 **A history of the Methodist Church in Ceylon, 1814-1964.**
Edited by Walter Joseph Tombleson Small.   Colombo: Wesley Press, 1971. 666p. bibliog.
The official history of the Methodist church, the origins of which are traced back to the Wesleyan Methodist missionaries who first arrived in Sri Lanka in 1814. The church's missionary activities and its important educational mission as well as the encounters between the Methodists and the state and other religious groups over the 150-year period are discussed.

223 **Christianity in Ceylon, its introduction and progress under the Portuguese, the Dutch, the British and American missions: with an historical sketch of the Brahaminical and Buddhist superstitions.**
James Emerson Tennent.   London: John Murray, 1850. 348p.
This work merits attention not only because of its effort to treat the history of Christianity in Sri Lanka in a comprehensive fashion but also because it exemplifies the attitudes which, by and large, prevailed among the Europeans respecting Buddhism and Hinduism.

Portuguese rule in Ceylon, 1594-1612.
See item no. 102.

A true and exact description of the Great Island of Ceylon.
See item no. 104.

The Catholic Church in Ceylon under Dutch rule.
See item no. 105.

The Portuguese rule in Ceylon, 1617-1638.
See item no. 106.

The temporal and spiritual conquest of Ceylon.
See item no. 114.

Sociology and anthropology of religion in Sri Lanka.
See item no. 204.

Christians of Ceylon and nationalist politics.
See item no. 284.

Islam

224   **Aspects of religion, economy and society among the Muslims of Ceylon.**
Mohamed Mauroof.   *Contributions to Indian Sociology*, new series, no. 6 (Dec. 1978), p. 67-83.

A sociologist's general discussion of the crucial importance of religion in the maintenance of the separate identity of the Muslims who have learned to adapt themselves to the life-style expectations of their non-Muslim neighbours. Also examines the economic significance of their trading activity, and social changes within the community.

225   **Some sociological aspects of the Muslim revivalism in Sri Lanka.**
Vijaya Samaraweera.   *Social Compass*, vol. 24, nos. 3-4 (1978), p. 465-75.

The late 19th-century religious and cultural revivalist movement among the Muslims is discussed in this essay in the context of its ideological and functional dimensions. Revivalism is identified as the crucial event in the emergence of the separate identity of the Muslims in modern Sri Lanka.

Collective identities, nationalisms and protest in modern Sri Lanka.
See item no. 300.

Muslim law in Ceylon: an historical outline.
See item no. 330.

Popular religious beliefs

226 **A celebration of demons: exorcism and the aesthetics of healing in Sri Lanka.**
Bruce Kapferer.   Bloomington, Indiana: Indiana University Press, 1983. 293p. map. bibliog.

An anthropological study of demonic illness and demonic ceremonies, including the cultural logic underlying major demonic ceremonies. Although written for the specialist, the general reader can glean an understanding of the exorcism rituals which have fascinated travellers to Sri Lanka over the years.

227 **The ceremonial dances of the Sinhalese: an inquiry into Sinhalese folk religion.**
Otaker Pertold.   Dehiwala, Sri Lanka: Tisara Prakasakayo, 1973. 142p. (*Ceylon Historical Journal*, vol. 20).

The famed Czech scholar's discussion of the significance of the ritual dances in relation to the ceremonies of invocation of deities of the Sinhalese. This was originally published in 1930 in *Archiv Oriental: Journal of the Czechoslovak Oriental Institute.*

228 **Exorcism and the art of healing in Ceylon.**
Paul Wirz.   Leiden, the Netherlands: Brill, 1954. 255p. bibliog.

A pioneering study of the folk beliefs of the Sinhalese of the Southwestern coastal belt. Myths of creation of demons and major exorcism rituals are described in detail and the author also examines the relationship between exorcism and healing in Sinhalese culture. This study was first published in German in 1941.

Modern Sri Lanka: a society in transition.
See item no. 5.

Sociology and anthropology of religion in Sri Lanka.
See item no. 204.

The karmic theater. Self, society and astrology in Jaffna.
See item no. 220.

Social Organization

Social groups
and social stratification

229 **Caste in Jaffna.**
Michael Y. Banks. In: *Aspects of Caste in South India, Ceylon and North West Pakistan*. Edited by Edmund Roland Leach. Cambridge, England: Cambridge University Press, 1960, p. 61-77. (Cambridge Papers in Social Anthropology, vol. 2).
An anthropologist's account of caste among the Tamils of Northern Sri Lanka and its role in kinship, marriage and inheritance.

230 **Vedda Villages of Anuradhapura. The historical anthropology of a community in Sri Lanka.**
James Brow. Seattle, Washington; London: University of Washington Press, 1978. 268p. 3 maps. bibliog. (Publications on Asia of the School of International Studies, no. 33).
An ethnography of the Veddas of Anuradhapura, an aboriginal community who have integrated themselves into the larger Sinhalese society but who nonetheless retain distinctive patterns of land usage, kinship, marriage and social customs.

231 **The Burghers of Ceylon.**
P. T. M. Fernando.   In: *The blending of races. Marginal identity in world perspectives*. Edited by Noel P. Grist, A. G. Dworkin. New York: Wiley, 1974, p. 61-78.

A sociological analysis of the Burghers, the descendants of Portuguese and Dutch settlers in Sri Lanka, who were closely identified with the ruling British in colonial times. The decline of their position and power in the post-independence years began to accelerate in the late 1950s when considerable numbers emigrated (principally to Australia and Canada) with the adoption of Sinhalese as the national language.

232 **Caste continuities in Ceylon. A study of the social structure of three tea plantations.**
Raja Jayaraman.   Bombay, India: Popular Prakahsan, 1975. 240p. 4 maps.

This sociological study (based on material collected in 1959-60) of the social structure of the Indian Tamil plantation workers and the enduring role played by caste among them is of importance, for it focuses on a group largely ignored in the scholarly literature. The volume is a revised version of a University of New Delhi doctoral thesis.

233 **Dutch Burghers and Portuguese mechanics: Eurasian ethnicity in Sri Lanka.**
Dennis Beaton McGilvray.   *Comparative Studies in Society and History*, vol. 24, no. 2 (April 1982), p. 235-63.

Explores the origins of the two elements of the Burgher community in Sri Lanka – the Dutch Burghers and Portuguese Burghers – and offers an ethnographic account of one group of Burghers, those in Batticaloa in the Eastern Province.

234 **Papers on the ethnography of Sri Lanka.**
Modern Ceylon Studies, vol. 4, nos. 1-2 (Jan.-July 1973), p. 1-127.

This special issue presents essays by six American scholars as embodying the new trends in the field of ethnography of Sri Lanka. Subjects covered are caste and matriclan structure in the Eastern Province, spatial organization and normative schemes in Jaffna, kinship as a system of rights, images of women in a Sinhalese myth, Christian and Buddhist symbols of evil, and Sinhalese colour terms. The authors write for the specialist reader.

235 **Caste in Tamil culture: the religious foundation of Sudra domin-
ation in Tamil Sri Lanka.**
Bryan Pfaffenberger. Syracuse, New York: Maxwell School of
Citizenship and Public Affairs, Syracuse University, 1982. 257p.
2 maps. bibliog. (Foreign and Comparative Studies/South Asian
Series, no. 7).

An anthropologist's study of the Vellalar who are not 'twice-born' but who
nonetheless enjoy the dominant place among the Tamils of Northern Sri Lanka.
The explanation for this is to be found in the Vellalar control of religious and
ritual practices. The study is flawed by its failure to take into account the
economic and political factors in the hierarchical ordering of Tamil society.

236 **Caste conflict and elite formation: the rise of a Karāva elite in Sri
Lanka, 1500-1931.**
Michael Roberts. Cambridge, England; New York: Cambridge
University Press, 1982. 382p. 7 maps. bibliog. (Cambridge South
Asian Studies, no. 24).

The emergence of the economic élite *par excellence* of Sri Lanka, the Karāva
élite, is the subject of this social history. It documents the integration of the
Karāva, an immigrant group from India, into the Sinhalese caste system, the
emergence of Karāva entrepreneurs, their remarkable achievements in the new
economy of British rule, the educational and professional attainments of the next
generation, and the struggle of the élite of the caste against their status inferior
position beginning in the later 19th century. The study digresses at times into
theoretical issues which are peripheral to it but it is a distinguished achievement,
remarkable especially for the range of sources it draws upon.

237 **Caste in modern Ceylon: the Sinhalese system in transition.**
Bryce Ryan. New Brunswick, New Jersey: Rutgers University
Press, 1953, 371p. map. bibliog.

As yet the only general work on caste among the Sinhalese, this study examines
caste from both historical and functional perspectives. The caste structure is
delineated and separate chapters consider caste in rural Sri Lanka and in the
urbanized setting where changes are occurring.

238 **The Veddas.**
Charles Gabriel Seligmann, Brenda Z. Seligmann. Cambridge,
England: Cambridge University Press, 1911. 463p. bibliog. map.

This classic ethnography offers the most comprehensive treatment of the Veddas,
the pre-Sinhalese aboriginal inhabitants of Sri Lanka. Some conclusions drawn by
the Seligmanns, in particular about the nature of the social organization of the
Veddas, have been questioned in recent years, but their study remains the pre-
eminent work in the field and it occupies an important place in the history of
social anthropology.

239 **A special caste? Tamil women of Sri Lanka.**
     Else Skjønsberg.   London: Zed Press, 1982. 143p. bibliog.
A sociologist's study of the determinants of sex roles among the Tamils of
Northern Sri Lanka, the position of Tamil women in the family, the way they
support themselves economically, and their unequal access to property, public
life, education, and health and welfare. The study is marred by serious flaws in its
theoretical approaches – specifically, its equating of caste with gender – and by
the author's polemical tone. Nonetheless, the volume is worthy of attention, for it
focuses on a subject which has not previously been studied in detail.

Sinhalese social organization: the Kandyan period.
See item no. 113.

History of Ceylon from the beginning of the nineteenth century to 1948.
See item no. 129.

**Some comments on the social backgrounds of the April 1971 insurgency in
Sri Lanka (Ceylon).**
See item no. 162.

The karmic theater. Self, society and astrology in Jaffna.
See item no. 220.

Kinship and marriage

240 **Pul Eliya. A village in Ceylon. A study of land tenure and kinship.**
     Edmund Roland Leach.   Cambridge, England: Cambridge
     University Press, 1961. 344p. 7 maps. bibliog.
A pioneering ethnography, this is a detailed study of the social system of a
Sinhalese village in the North Central Province, with particular attention devoted
to the land tenurial arrangements, kinship and the organization and rewards of
labour.

241 **Under the Bo tree: studies in caste, kinship and marriage in the
     interior of Ceylon.**
     Nur Yalman.   Berkeley, California; Los Angeles; London:
     University of California Press, 1971. Paperback ed. 406p. 12 maps.
     bibliog.
An important anthropological study based on field work in a Kandyan dry zone
village. The castes and patterns of kinship and marriage are detailed. There is a
comparison of these patterns with those in other communities in Sri Lanka as well
as in South India, with the author developing a framework of common principles
to understand the thought and behaviour of the different communities observed.

Sinhalese social organization: the Kandyan period.
See item no. 113.

Law and the marriage relationship in Sri Lanka.
See item no. 339.

Land tenure in village Ceylon: a sociological and historical study.
See item no. 413.

Social change and social problems

242 **The liberation of the village.**
Edited by Centre for Society and Religion. Colombo: Centre for Society and Religion, 1977. 214p.

A collection of essays with an activist thrust on the socio-economic problems facing Sri Lankan villages. Issues regarding health and transport receive special treatment and a series of essays address the role which socialism could play in transforming rural Sri Lanka.

243 **Status integration and suicide in Ceylon.**
Jack P. Gibbs, Walter T. Martin. *American Journal of Sociology*, vol. 64, no. 6 (May 1969), p. 585-91.

The authors argue that the high rate of suicide in Sri Lanka confirms the theory that the suicide rate of a population varies inversely with the degree of status integration and posit further that these suicides conform to the 'egoistic' model rathern than to the 'altruistic'.

244 **Survival with integrity: Sarvodaya at the crossroads.**
Dennis Goulet, introduction by Godfrey Gunatilleke. Colombo: Marga Institute, in association with the Overseas Development Council, Washington, 1981. 105p.

An examination of the views on national development of Sarvodaya, the village development movement begun in 1958, in relation to the policies of the United National Party government since 1977. The author questions the viability of the movement's alternative strategies for development given its dependence upon foreign assistance for their successful implementation.

245 **Criminal homicide in the Southern Province.**
C. H. S. Jayawardene, H. Ranasinghe. Colombo: Colombo Apothecaries, 1963. 181p. 8 maps. bibliog.

A pioneer study, which emphasizes the important role played by the modernization processes in the incidence of criminal homicide in one of the most populous regions of Sri Lanka.

246 **Report of the Kandyan Peasantry Commission.**
Kandyan Peasantry Commission. Colombo: Ceylon Government Press, 1951. 529p. 13 maps. (Sessional Paper XVIII of 1951).

An important and influential report of the committee appointed by the government to investigate the social and economic conditions of the Kandyan peasantry. The report is wide ranging – subjects covered include land holding, housing, education, communications, medical care, employment and social services – but it is particularly noteworthy for its explicit support for the long-held popular view that the plight of the Kandyan peasantry is to be attributed to the establishment and expansion of plantations during British rule.

247 **Sarvodaya. The other development.**
Detlef Kantowsky. New Delhi: Vikas, 1980. 228p. bibliog.

Sarvodaya in Sri Lanka is examined in this study at two levels, as a concept and as a concept in practice. The author also compares the Sri Lanka movement to the older Sarvodaya movement in India – which is discussed in detail – and its distinguishing features, principally its links with Buddhism, are delineated.

248 **The spiral of suicide and social change in Sri Lanka.**
Robert N. Kearney, Barbara D. Miller. *Journal of Asian Studies*, vol. 45, no. 1 (Nov. 1985), p. 81-101.

This essay is concerned with a disturbing phenomenon in contemporary Sri Lanka, the high rate of suicides. Incidence and changes in the incidence of suicide by age group, sex and region are examined for indications as to which categories of persons within the society appear to be most vulnerable to suicide. Data covers the period 1955-1978.

249 **Dharma and development. Religion as resource in the Sarvodaya movement.**
Joanna Macy, introduction by Ahangamage Tudor Ariyaratna.
West Hartford, Connecticut: Kumarian Press, 1983. 102p. map. bibliog. (K. P. Development Monograph, no. 2).

Exemplifying Sarvodaya, the author argues that, to enlist popular participation and commitment, development programmes should have a value-base that is meaningful to the people and that these values can be found in the indigenous religious traditions. The author's clear identification with Sarvodaya colours her assessment of its successes and failures. The introduction is by the founder of Sarvodaya.

250 **The disintegrating village: social change in rural Sri Lanka.**
Edited by Barrie M. Morrison, Michael P. Moore, M. U. Ishak Lebbe. Colombo: Lake House Investments, 1979. 273p.

Case studies of six villages, exploring the theme of modernization, form the basis for generalizations about rural Sri Lanka. The representativeness of the villages is questionable, and the contributors' use of the concept of 'modernization', which has been widely criticized for its conceptual weaknesses, raises questions about the appropriateness of the analytic framework adopted for the case studies.

68

251   The wrong end of the rope. Women coir workers in Sri Lanka.
       Carla Risseeuw.   Leiden, the Netherlands: Research Project
       Women and Development, 1980. 253p. map. bibliog.

This work reports the results of a participant observation study carried out among
the women in a village in the Southwestern coastal belt of Sri Lanka whose
traditional occupation is coir rope-making. The life and work of the rope-makers
are examined within the context of changing economic and social conditions. This
work merits special attention because it constitutes one of the few detailed studies
available on women in contemporary Sri Lanka.

252   A woman's mind is longer than a kitchen spoon. Report on women
       in Sri Lanka.
       Carla Risseeuw, Dharma Wickremasinghe, El Postel, Joke
       Schrijvers.   Leiden, the Netherlands: Research Project Women
       and Development and Rijksuniversiteit; Colombo: National
       Institute of Business Management, 1980. 146p. map. bibliog.

This report embodies the research work undertaken by a Sri Lankan-Dutch team
which investigated, with the goal of formulating policy recommendations, the
impact of change and development on Sri Lankan women and their practical
experiences. Although much valuable material is presented here, the reader
should be aware that the authors' unfamiliarity with the recent literature on Sri
Lanka has resulted in serious problems of interpretation in some areas.

253   Sinhalese village.
       Bryce Ryan, in collaboration with L. D. Jayasena, D. C. R.
       Wickremasinghe.   Coral Gables, Florida: University of Miami
       Press, 1958. 229p. 2 maps. bibliog.

A pioneering 'village study', this sociological account examines in detail a village
in the Southwestern coastal belt, devoting particular attention to the socio-
economic changes which confronted it.

254   The process of dynamisation in rural Ceylon, with special reference
       to a Kandyan village in transition.
       Theodor von Fellenberg.   Bern: A. E. Bruderer, 1966. 242p.
       bibliog.

Focusing largely on the self-help efforts in a Kandyan village, the author examines
the process of dynamisation in rural Sri Lanka and identifies both internal and
external factors in the dynamisation. The author's preoccupation with delineating
all the possible factors in the dynamization has resulted in what is best described
as superficial discussions in some sections of the book.

255 **Youth in Ceylon.**
C. P. Wijesinghe. In: *Youth: a transcultural psychiatric approach.*
Edited by Jules Masserman. New York: Grune & Stratton, 1969,
p. 31-44.

The youth of Sri Lanka, their role in society and the problems they have faced as
a result of social changes are discussed in this essay by a psychiatrist.

256 **Crime and aggression in changing Ceylon: a sociological analysis of
homicide, suicide and economic crime.**
Arthur Lewis Wood. *Transactions of the American Philosophical
Society*, new series, vol. 51, part 8 (1961), p. 1-132.

Using the Sinhalese Buddhist villagers of the Southwest as the subjects, the
author discusses the social and cultural determinants of major crime and suicide in
Sri Lanka in the period 1925 to 1960. Though not without drawbacks – for
example, some of the author's underlying assumptions about the cultural values of
the Sinhalese are to be questioned – this work deserves recognition as the most
comprehensive study as yet undertaken on the strikingly high rates of serious
crimes and suicide among the Sinhalese.

Modern Sri Lanka: a society in transition.
See item no. 5.

History of Ceylon from the beginning of the nineteenth century to 1948.
See item no. 129.

**Some comments on the social backgrounds of the April 1971 insurgency in
Sri Lanka (Ceylon).**
See item no. 162.

The cult of goddess Pattini.
See item no. 206.

Land tenure in village Ceylon: a sociological and historical study.
See item no. 413.

Social Services, Health and Welfare

257 **Socioeconomic determinants of child malnutrition in Sri Lanka: the evidence from Galle and Kalutara Districts.**
Senaka Abeyratne, Thomas T. Poleman. Ithaca, New York: Department of Agricultural Economics, New York State College of Agriculture and Life Sciences, 1983. 76p. bibliog. (Cornell International Agricultural Economics Study, no. 18).
This extended essay examines the issue of child malnutrition within the framework of Sri Lanka's nutrition policy.

258 **Health policy and politics in Sri Lanka. Developments in the South Asian welfare state.**
J. W. Bjorkman. *Asian Survey*, vol. 25, no. 5 (May 1985), p. 537-52.
This essay draws attention to an important subject, the process of policy-making in the health care field and its relationship to the broader political framework.

259 **Sri Lanka: doctors in the Colombo General Hospital.**
Malsiri Dias. In: *Doctors and society. Three Asian case studies*. Edited by T. N. Madan. New Delhi: Vikas, 1980, p. 211-78.
The only study of its kind, this is an evaluation of the part played by institution-based medical practice in the development process. Two hundred and twenty-five doctors were studied and the author discusses the training and aspirations of the doctors, and the interaction of cultural and 'underdevelopment' factors in their professionalism. The author concludes that the doctors are unaware of the attitudes, beliefs and cultural practices of their patients, and that they cling to their more traditional role of specialist in treatment and have been slow in reconsidering their role to meet the changing needs of the country.

260 **Cooperative societies in developing nations: some problems at the grass-roots as seen in four Sri Lankan villages.**
Tissa Fernando. *Plural Societies*, vol. 7, no. 2 (1976), p. 33-47.

Provides valuable insights into the working of cooperatives in Sri Lanka. The author questions in particular the validity of state cooption of the cooperatives to achieve its goals since it has an adverse impact on popular participation, and points out how cooperatives have been used by the élite to dominate rural society.

261 **Country resource utilization review: Sri Lanka.**
Health Resources Group for Primary Health Care, World Health Organization. Geneva: World Health Organization, 1982. 55p.

A critical review of medical policy and public health in Sri Lanka, with a discussion of the cost of medical care and the issue of international medical cooperation.

262 **Cooperation: its rise and growth in Ceylon.**
G. Kurukulasuriya. Colombo: Co-operative Federation of Ceylon, 1971. 311p. map. bibliog.

A detailed but uncritical examination of the development of the cooperative movement in Sri Lanka.

263 **Needs of children and adolescents. A case study of Sri Lanka.**
Marga Institute. Colombo: Marga Institute, 1975. 166p.

This study, undertaken on behalf of the United Nations Children's Fund, examines the needs of Sri Lanka's children and adolescents in terms of formal education, non-formal education, health, and sports and recreation. A lengthy appendix contains supporting statistical data.

264 **Housing in Sri Lanka.**
Marga Institute. Colombo: Marga Institute, 1976. 255p. (Marga Research Studies – 6).

A comprehensive study of housing developments in Sri Lanka since the mid-1950s, with an evaluation of the future housing needs in both the urban and rural sectors.

265 **Notes on the medical topography of the interior of Ceylon; and on the health of the troops employed in the Kandyan Provinces, during the years 1815, 1816, 1817, 1818, 1819 and 1820: with brief remarks on the prevailing diseases.**
Henry Marshall. London: Burgess & Hill; Dublin: Hodges & M'Arthur; Edinburgh: Adam Black, 1821. 228p.

The author of this classic work went to Sri Lanka in 1808 as an Assistant-Surgeon in the British army and became the senior medical officer in the Kandyan Provinces after the cession of the Kandyan kingdom to the British in 1815, a position he was to hold until 1821.

266 **The cultural background of Sinhalese medicine.**
Gananath Obeyesekere. *Journal of Anthropological Survey of India*, vol. 4 (1969), p. 117-39.

Arguing that the traditional (*ayurvedic*) medicine of the Sinhalese cannot be meaningfully understood in terms of Western science, the author examines the cultural background of *ayurveda* and discusses the factors which explain its acceptance by the Sinhalese.

267 **The impact of Ayurvedic ideas on the culture and individual.**
Gananath Obeyesekere. In: *Asian medical systems: a comparative study*. Edited by Charles Leslie. Berkeley, California; Los Angeles: University of California Press, 1976, p. 201-26.

In this essay, which makes a valuable contribution to the understanding of the role and place of *ayurveda* (traditional medicine) among the Sinhalese, the author also discusses the broader cultural acceptance of *ayurvedic* ideas and describes what he identifies as cultural diseases.

268 **Illness, culture, and meaning: some comments on the nature of traditional medicine.**
Gananath Obeyesekere. In: *Culture and healing in Asian societies: anthropological, psychiatric and public health studies*. Edited by Arthur Kleinman, Peter Kunstadter, E. Russell Alexander, Jane L. Gale. Cambridge, Massachusetts: Schenkman, 1978, p. 253-64.

Examines traditional (*ayurvedic*) medicine as practised in contemporary Sri Lanka and draws attention to its importance in relation to the inability of Western medicine to deal with certain kinds of illnesses and disease.

269 **Health, politics and social change in Sri Lanka.**
K. N. Seneviratne. *Round Table*, no. 280 (Oct. 1980), p. 389-400.

A discussion of Sri Lanka's achievements in the health care field since the 1930s and an analysis of the major problems faced by health care planners since the 1960s. Includes data on health care which is not otherwise easily accessible to the general reader.

Basic needs, poverty and government policies in Sri Lanka.
See item no. 367.

Dismantling welfarism in Sri Lanka.
See item no. 376.

Social Services, Health and Welfare

Welfare and growth in Sri Lanka: a case study of Sri Lanka prepared for the UNRISD project 'the unified approach to development planning & analysis'.
See item no. 378.

A bibliography on health in Sri Lanka, 1979-1980.
See item no. 630.

Majority-Minority Relations

270 **Nationalism, communalism, and national unity in Sri Lanka.**
Sinnappah Arasaratnam.   In: *India and Ceylon: unity and diversity, a symposium*. Edited by Philip Mason. London, New York: Oxford University Press for Institute of Race Relations, 1967, p. 260-78.

Surveys the rise of Sinhalese-Buddhist nationalism and its impact upon the English-educated élite's power and status and upon the communal and religious minorities. The author argues that Sinhalese nationalism had reached its peak and that minorities had learnt to moderate their demands. Subsequent developments, of course, proved the author wrong but this essay is still of value, for it reflects the optimism which prevailed in the mid-1960s among the élite that the sectional interests and loyalties of conflicting types that emerged in independent Sri Lanka lacked the capacity to undermine its national unity.

271 **Race relations in Sri Lanka.**
Edited by Centre for Society and Religion.   Colombo: Centre for Society and Religion, 1978. 262p.

This collection, brought together by the well-known Roman Catholic Church-oriented activist centre, presents essays by leading Sri Lankan public figures, documents and basic information which pertain to Sinhalese-Tamil relations. The essays, written with the general reader in mind, exemplify what is best described as the 'liberal' approach to the communal conflict.

272 **Sri Lanka: the ethnic conflict: myths, realities and perspectives.**
Committee for Rational Development.   Delhi: Navarang, 1985.

A collection of documents, statements and essays relating to Sinhalese-Tamil relations. The documents are invaluable for an understanding of the relative positions of the two ethnic groups in government employment, education, the

75

professions and the economy. The essays, which are of varying quality, offer analyses of the ethnic conflict from both Left and what is best described as 'Liberal' perspectives. H.A.I. Goonetileke's bibliography entitled 'July 1983 and the national question in Sri Lanka', which is included in the volume, has also been published separately (*see* item no. 627).

273 **Discrimination in Sri Lanka.**
Kingsley Muthumuni de Silva. In: *Case studies on human rights and fundamental freedom: a world survey.* Edited by W. A. Veenhaven. The Hague: Nijhoff, 1975-76, vol. 3, p. 71-119.

Placing the issue of discrimination within the context of Sri Lanka's plural society, the author discusses discrimination suffered by minorities as a result of the triumph of Sinhalese linguistic nationalism during the period 1956 to 1976 as well as discrimination practised on the basis of caste and gender.

274 **Managing ethnic tensions in multi-ethnic societies: Sri Lanka 1880-1985.**
Kingsley Muthumuni de Silva. Lanham, Maryland: University Press of America on behalf of the Institute of Asian Affairs, Hamburg, and the International Center for Ethnic Studies, Kandy/Colombo, Sri Lanka, 1986. 434p. 3 maps. bibliog.

This detailed and comprehensive historical study of the relations between the majority Sinhalese and the minority communities is divided into three parts. The first part examines issues of ethnic relations in the period up to 1952 within the context of nationalism, constitutional reform and the transfer of power. The second part discusses the triumph of linguistic nationalism, and the final part focuses on ethnic conflict and political development from 1972 to 1985. This study is of particular value because of its consideration of the issue of ethnicity not only in terms of Sinhalese-Tamil relations but also in terms of the other minority communities – its treatment of the Muslims and their relations with both the Sinhalese and Tamils is especially noteworthy.

275 **The agony of Sri Lanka: an in-depth account of the racial riots of 1983.**
T. D. S. A. Dissanayaka. Colombo: Swastika, 1983. 120p.

A detailed description of the events of July 1983 which is worthy of attention because the writer releases information he was privy to as a senior government official.

276 **Ceylon: a divided nation.**
Bertram Hughes Farmer. London: Oxford University Press for Institute of Race Relations, 1963. 74p. 2 maps.

Succinctly examines ethnic tensions and their historical causes.

277 **Communalism and language in the politics of Ceylon.**
Robert N. Kearney. Durham, North Carolina: Duke University
Press, 1967. 165p. map. bibliog. (Program in Comparative Studies
on South Asia, no. 2).

Focusing on the centrally important language issue, the author examines the
relationship between the majority Sinhalese and the minority Tamils within the
framework of post-independent Sri Lanka's political process. Appendixes provide
the principal official documents which pertain to the language issue, from 1956 to
1966.

278 **Language and the rise of Tamil separatism in Sri Lanka.**
Robert N. Kearney. *Asian Survey*, vol. 18, no. 5 (May 1978),
p. 521-34.

A succinct analysis of the emergence and crystallization of separatist sentiments
among the Tamils, emphasizing the crucial role language played in the self-
identification of both the Tamils and Sinhalese.

279 **The cultural dimension of Tamil separatism in Sri Lanka.**
Bryan Pfaffenberger. *Asian Survey*, vol. 21, no. 11 (Nov. 1981),
p. 1,145-57.

Argues that the separatist sentiments among the Tamils have been animated not
only by concerns about their material well-being in the Sinhalese-dominated
polity but also by the profound pride they take in their cultural tradition. This
tradition, it is pointed out, favours the dominance of the conservative and
powerful Vellalar caste and to that extent questions necessarily have to be raised
about the status and place of lower castes and other marginal groups in a Vellalar-
dominated state.

280 **The Tamils of Sri Lanka.**
Walter Schwartz. London: Minority Rights Group, 1979. Rev.
ed. 16p. map. bibliog. (MRG Report, no. 25).

An overview of the grievances of the Tamils, both Sri Lankan and Indian, against
the majority Sinhalese.

281 **Sri Lanka. Ethnic fratricide and the dismantling of democracy.**
Stanley Jeyaraj Tambiah. Chicago; London: University of
Chicago Press, 1986. 198p. map.

The distinguished Sri Lankan anthropologist's searching examination of the
factors that combined to produce the tragic and explosive stage which Sinhalese-
Tamil relations reached by mid-1984. As the author defines it, this is an 'engaged
political tract' and not a 'distanced academic treatise' but it is not a polemical or
propagandist piece and it merits careful reading by those concerned with
contemporary Sri Lanka.

282   Emergency '58: the story of the Ceylon race riots.
      Tarzie Vittachi.   London: Deutsch, 1958. 124p. map.
A journalist's account of the first major Sinhalese-Tamil ethnic conflict of
independent Sri Lanka. It is particularly valuable for the description it offers of
the indecisiveness of the government in the face of the violence.

283   The states of South Asia: problems of national integration. Essays in
      honour of W. H. Morris-Jones.
      Edited by Alfred Jeyaratnam Wilson, Dennis Dalton.   London:
      C. Hurst, 1982. 343p.
The contributions on Sri Lanka are K. M. de Silva's discussion of the transfer of
power in 1948, C. R. de Silva's essay on the Sinhalese-Tamil rift and A. J.
Wilson's consideration of the future of Sri Lanka in relation to the conflict
between the Sinhalese and Tamils.

Tamils of Sri Lanka. Their history and role.
See item no. 89.

Kingdom of Jaffna, part 1 (circa. 1250-1450).
See item no. 97.

History of Ceylon from the beginning of the nineteenth century to 1948.
See item no. 129.

1915 Riots in Ceylon: a symposium.
See item no. 144.

**Elite conflict in Sri Lanka and Sinhalese perspectives: barriers to
accommodation.**
See item no. 151.

Sri Lanka since independence.
See item no. 158.

Sri Lanka in change and crisis.
See item no. 161.

**The revolt in the temple composed to commemorate 2500 years of the
land, the race and the faith.**
See item no. 163.

Ceylon: dilemmas of a new nation.
See item no. 165.

**Nativism, diglossia and the Sinhalese identity in the language problem in
Sri Lanka.**
See item no. 180.

A standard language and socio-historical parameters: standard Sri Lankan Tamil.
See item no. 190.

The Kataragama pilgrimage: Hindu-Buddhist interaction and its significance in Sri Lanka's polyethnic social system.
See item no. 207.

Religion and legitimation of power in Sri Lanka.
See item no. 216.

Collective identities, nationalisms and protest in modern Sri Lanka.
See item no. 300.

The politics of language in India and Ceylon.
See item no. 306.

Weightage in university admissions. Standardization and district quotas in Sri Lanka.
See item no. 454.

The politics of university admissions: a review of some aspects of the admissions policy in Sri Lanka, 1971-1978.
See item no. 455.

July 1983 and the national question in Sri Lanka: a bibliographical guide.
See item no. 627.

Politics

284 **Christians of Ceylon and nationalist politics.**
Sinnappah Arasaratnam. In: *Religion in South Asia. Religious
conversion and revival movements in South Asia in mediaeval and
modern times.* Edited by G. A. Oddie. New Delhi: Manohar
Book Service, 1977, p. 163-82.
An historical survey of the role of the Christian community in Sri Lanka's political
process.

285 **A statistical survey of elections to the legislatures of Sri Lanka,
1911-1977.**
G. P. S. Harischandra de Silva. Colombo: Marga Institute, 1979.
439p. 4 maps. bibliog.
This compilation brings together data found in scattered official documents and
presents a basic statistical analysis of the election results and information about
the membership of the national legislature during the period covered.

286 **Universal franchise, 1931-1981: the Sri Lankan experience.**
Edited by Kingsley Muthumuni de Silva. Colombo: Department
of Information, 1981. 254p. 5 maps. bibliog.
A collective critical examination of Sri Lanka's experience of universal franchise
and the background to its introduction. A statistical appendix provides
demographic and electoral data from 1947 to 1977. The electoral delimitations are
represented in the maps.

287 **Elite politics in the new states: the case of independent Sri Lanka.**
Tissa Fernando. *Pacific Affairs*, no. 46 (Fall 1973), p. 361-83.
In this penetrating analysis of the élite power structure in Sri Lanka, the author explores in particular the reasons for the remarkable success the élites have had in maintaining their dominance within the framework of a parliamentary system.

288 **A short history of the Lanka Sama Samaja Party.**
Leslie Goonewardene. Colombo: Gunaratne, 1961. 66p.
The official history of the Trotskyite political party, the largest and most important Leftist political organization in Sri Lanka. The period covered is from 1935 to 1960.

289 **The Ceylon general election in 1947.**
William Ivor Jennings. *University of Ceylon Review*, vol. 6, no. 3 (July 1948), p. 133-94.
This detailed study of the election for independent Sri Lanka's first parliament examines the political parties, constituencies, candidates, electoral campaigns, and the results of the polls.

290 **Additional notes on the general election of 1952.**
William Ivor Jennings. *Ceylon Historical Journal*, vol. 2, nos. 3-4 (Jan. Apr. 1953), p. 193-208.
A continuation of the analysis provided by I. D. S. Weerawardana in *The general elections in Ceylon, 1952* (q.v.).

291 **Caste and family in the politics of the Sinhalese, 1947-1976.**
Janice Jiggins. Cambridge, England: Cambridge University Press, 1979. 189p. 7 maps. bibliog.
This study of the two forces which the author delineates as being critical in animating the politics of the Sinhalese is flawed by the failure to provide theoretical definitions of both caste and family and by the use of questionable statistical methods. The greater emphasis is on the role of caste, and electoral data are discussed to assert that caste is the major determinant of voter behaviour. The role of the family in politics is examined in relation to the principal families associated with the two main political parties, the United National Party and the Sri Lanka Freedom Party. There is also a chapter devoted to the 1971 April Insurrection.

292 **Sri Lanka: third world democracy.**
James Jupp. London: Cass, 1978. 423p. 2 maps. bibliog. (Studies in Commonwealth History and Politics, no. 6).
Focusing on the institutional framework of post-independent Sri Lanka's politics, this study offers a detailed discussion of party organization, opinion and pressure groups, the electoral system, the working of the transplanted institutions, and the changes the political system has faced. Minority politics is also considered in some

detail. Less attention has been paid to the social and economic forces operative in the polity at large and to their role in politics. Appendixes provide national election results from 1947 to 1977, and national results broken down on a regional basis from 1960 to 1977.

293　**The Marxist parties of Ceylon.**
　　　Robert N. Kearney. In: *Radical politics in South Asia.* Edited by
　　　Paul R. Brass, Marcus Franda.　Cambridge, Massachusetts: MIT
　　　Press, 1973, p. 401-39.

Surveys the development of the Marxist parties since the mid-1930s and discusses the structure and organization of the two principal Marxist parties, the Lanka Sama Samaja Party and the Communist Party, and their role in post-independent Sri Lanka's political process.

294　**The politics of Ceylon (Sri Lanka).**
　　　Robert N. Kearney.　Ithaca, New York, London: Cornell
　　　University Press, 1973. 249p. bibliog.

A useful general survey of the political processes and institutions of post-independent Sri Lanka up to 1973. Intended for the non-specialist, it examines the historical background, governmental institutions, political parties, education, communal politics and the challenges faced by the political order. An introductory guide to research on Sri Lankan politics is also included.

295　**Women in politics in Sri Lanka.**
　　　Robert N. Kearney.　*Asian Survey*, vol. 21, no. 7 (July 1981),
　　　p. 729-46.

Despite the achievements of some prominent political women, few women have chosen to enter the political life, and women represented in the national legislature have not exceeded four percent of its membership over the last three decades. The explanation for this is to be found, the author argues, in the firmly embedded notion in the ethos of the society that a woman's central concern is the home and family.

296　**Origins of Trotskyism in Ceylon. A documentary history of the
　　　Lanka Sama Samaja Party, 1935-1942.**
　　　George Jan Lerski.　Stanford, California: Hoover Institute for
　　　War, Revolution and Peace, 1968. 288p. bibliog.

Studies the origins of the Lanka Sama Samaja Party in the mid-1930s and its development up to the Second World War period when its future became clouded by the threat of government repression and by conflicts within the leadership over the issue of the party's attitude towards the Soviet Union.

297 **The state and peasant politics in Sri Lanka.**
Mick Moore.   Cambridge, England: Cambridge University Press,
1985. 326p. 4 maps. bibliog.

Perhaps the most important study of contemporary politics to be published in
recent years, this work is concerned with explaining why a highly politicised rural
electorate which has played a major role in replacing governments at successive
general elections has not used its electoral power to advocate and advance its
interests at the national level. Arguing that the Sri Lankan peasantry has been
inducted into electoral political participation on the basis of identities other than
that of the agricultural producer, the author examines the failure of the peasantry
to realise a class identity in national politics in terms of the relationship between
interests and demands as formulated within the framework of a polity dominated
by the élite.

298 **Legislators and representation in Sri Lanka. The decentralization of
development planning.**
Robert C. Oberst.   Boulder, Colorado; London: Westview, 1985.
157p. bibliog. (Westview Special Studies on South and Southeast
Asia).

Explores the relationship between Sri Lankan legislators and their constituents
and argues that representation is an interactive process, necessarily involving both
parties, and that this process has contributed to the political stability of the
country. The title of this monograph is misleading, for the subject of
decentralization of development planning is treated only in one chapter.

299 **Religion and politics in Sri Lanka.**
Urmila Phadnis.   New Delhi: Manohar Book Service; Columbia,
Missouri: South Asia Books, 1976. 376p. bibliog.

Studies the interplay of religion and politics in the history of Sri Lanka. The
precolonial and colonial periods are treated in summary fashion. The post-
independent period receives detailed attention and the involvement of Buddhist
monks in such 'political' issues as language, land reform and foreign policy is
examined at length. The failure to explain the wider setting of the political
process of which the Buddhist monks became a part is a major drawback, and the
perceptions of the Buddhists themselves of the legitimacy of the activism of the
Buddhist monks has not received the attention it deserves. The study is concerned
only with Buddhism.

300 **Collective identities, nationalisms and protest in modern Sri Lanka.**
Edited by Michael Roberts.   Colombo: Marga Institute, 1979.
573p. 10 maps. bibliog.

This collection of essays offers the most comprehensive treatment of political
ideologies and movements in modern Sri Lanka. The volume is divided into four
parts: the first is devoted to background and roots, the second to the emergence
of collective identity in colonial times, the third to British attitudes towards
nationalism and transfer of power, and the last to developments in post-
independent Sri Lanka.

301 **Political structure in a changing Sinhalese village.**
Marguerite S. Robinson. Cambridge, England: Cambridge
University Press, 1975. 376p. 4 maps. bibliog. (Cambridge South
Asian Studies, no. 15).

The nature of political change in a Kandyan highland village from the immediate
pre-independent period to the late 1960s is considered. The author devotes
particular attention to the role played by the Sri Lanka Freedom Party
government after 1956 in the politicization of the village and the resultant
structural change from a situation in which village solidarity transcended
individual political preference to one in which political party identification became
paramount.

302 **Sri Lanka's 1977 general election: the resurgence of the UNP.**
Vijaya Samaraweera. *Asian Survey*, vol. 17, no. 12 (Dec. 1977),
p. 1,195-1206.

This essay discusses the new electoral delimitation and the election campaigns of
the major political parties and analyses the election results. Explanations are
provided for the remarkable triumph of the United National Party (UNP) and the
débâcle of the Sri Lanka Freedom Party and the Marxist parties.

303 **Sri Lankan Marxists in electoral politics, 1947-1977.**
Vijaya Samaraweera. *Journal of Commonwealth & Comparative
Politics*, vol. 18, no. 3 (Nov. 1980), p. 308-24.

The nature and extent of the support drawn by the traditional Marxist parties in
electoral politics is examined. Two principal conclusions are presented: firstly,
that it is not class interest but rather the personality of the leaders and the
organizational strength of the parties which account for the Marxists' electoral
successes; and secondly, that the electoral alliances which the Marxists entered
into with the Sri Lanka Freedom Party worked to their detriment at the polls.

304 **The emerging elite. A study of political leadership in Ceylon.**
Marshall R. Singer. Cambridge, Massachusetts: MIT Press, 1964.
203p. bibliog.

The emergence of the modern political élite in Sri Lanka is the subject of this
study and it concludes that the élite is a middle class élite representing the middle
class but that it has also succeeded in identifying itself with the interests of the
Sinhalese population at large. Questionable biographical data on some élite
figures mars this study.

305 **South Asian politics and religion.**
Edited by Donald Eugene Smith. Princeton, New Jersey:
Princeton University Press, 1966. 563p.

Part four of this volume is devoted to Sri Lanka. D. E. Smith's two essays
examine, respectively, the triumph of Buddhist populism with the electoral
success of the S. W. R. D. Bandaranaike-led Mahajana Eksath Peramuna in 1956
and the role of 'political monks' in monastic reform. A. J. Wilson discusses the

place of Buddhism in the political process of Sri Lanka between 1960 and 1965, and in the final essay, C. D. S. Siriwardane offers an historical survey of Buddhist reorganization.

306 **The politics of language in India and Ceylon.**
Stanley Jeyaraj Tambiah. *Modern Asian Studies*, vol. 1, no. 3 (July 1967), p. 215-40.
The primary focus of this essay is on India but the discussion on the politics of language in independent Sri Lanka and its implications for ethnic relations is worthy of attention.

307 **Recent politics in Sri Lanka: the presidential election and the referendum of 1982. A study of electoral politics and behaviour in an Asian democracy.**
W. A. Wiswa Warnapala, L. Dias Hewagama. New Delhi: Navarang, 1983. 240p. bibliog.
The two key political developments in Sri Lanka in 1982, the presidential election won by J. R. Jayewardene, and the referendum, the passing of which enabled the United National Party to extend the life of Parliament for a further full term, are critically examined in this study. The authors express grave concern about the governing party's commitment to democracy, although their clear partisan stance brings their objectivity into question.

308 **The general elections in Ceylon, 1952.**
I. D. S. Weerawardana. *Ceylon Historical Journal*, vol. 2, nos. 1-2 (July-Oct. 1952), p. 109-72.
The most detailed analysis available of the 1952 general election.

309 **Ceylon general election 1956.**
I. D. S. Weerawardana. Colombo: M. D. Gunasena, 1960. 262p. bibliog.
A political scientist's careful assessment of the general elections of 1956 which brought about the first change of government in Sri Lanka since independence. The political parties, candidates and their constituencies, the issues, the electoral campaign, and the results are examined in detail.

310 **Electoral politics in an emergent state – the Ceylon general election of May 1970.**
Alfred Jeyaratnam Wilson. Cambridge, England: Cambridge University Press, 1975. 240p. 2 maps. bibliog. (Perspectives on Development, no. 3).
This study offers a detailed description and anlaysis of the 1970 election, following the methodology of the Nuffield studies of British general elections. The author's access to the leaders of the political parties has provided him with illuminating material. On the other hand, the absence of surveys of voter opinion in the

discussions on voter attitudes and perceptions is a major drawback. Detailed statistics pertaining to the 1970 election and data on the past electoral behaviour of the Sri Lankans are included.

311 Socialism in Sri Lanka.

Alfred Jeyaratnam Wilson. In: *Socialism in the Third World*. Edited by Helen Desfosses, Jacques Levesque. New York: Praeger, 1975, p. 255-90. (Praeger Special Studies in International Politics and Government).

This survey of developments since the 1930s is a useful introduction to socialism in Sri Lanka. The author emphasizes the importance of some commitment to socialist goals on the part of political parties vying for parliamentary power in the context of voter expectations. These commitments and changes in the commitments are examined, revealing that socialism in Sri Lanka covers a wide ideological spectrum. Special attention is devoted to the traditional Marxist parties which embraced parliamentary democracy, and the challenges they faced in the 1970s with the emergence of a new Left with a commitment to revolutionary action.

312 Politics in Sri Lanka, 1947-1979.

Alfred Jeyaratnam Wilson. London: Macmillan, 1979. 2nd ed. 320p. 2 maps. bibliog.

This study, by the best known of the Sri Lankan political scientists, is now recognized as the standard work on the politics of post-independent Sri Lanka. Placing politics within a wider framework, the author addresses a wide range of subjects which bear upon his central concerns, political forces and political behaviour. Thus, separate chapters deal with the land and its people, problems of a plural society, and economic and social progress, as well as with the constitution and government, and foreign policy and defence agreements. The major criticism of this study is that it often tends to be descriptive rather than analytical.

313 The growth of a party system in Ceylon.

Calvin A. Woodward. Providence, Rhode Island: Brown University Press, 1969. 338p. map. bibliog.

The parliamentary elections from 1947 to 1965 form the framework within which the emergence of a competitive party system and the corresponding decline of personality parties and independent candidates in the electoral arena are examined. The focus of the study is on the national scene and the intriguing question of the relationship between national and local politics and its implications for the development of the party system has not attracted the author's attention. Statistical analyses of the electoral data supplement the text and there is a useful annotated list of the major political parties and their leaders.

314   **Youth protest in Sri Lanka (Ceylon).**
      W. Howard Wriggins, C. H. S. Jayawardene. In: *Population
      politics and the future of Southern Asia.* Edited by W. Howard
      Wriggins, James F. Guyot.   New York, London: Columbia
      University Press, 1973, p. 318-50.

Exemplifying the April 1971 Insurrection, the authors consider the relationship
between demographic change and political protest on the part of youth. The
marked increase in the numbers of the youth, their changing values, and their
high rate of unemployment are examined as causal factors of the insurrection and
the authors rightly stress the crucial importance of the ability of the leadership of
the Janatha Vimukti Peramuna to mobilize support for the revolutionary cause.

Sri Lanka: a survey.
See item no. 4.

Modern Sri Lanka: a society in transition.
See item no. 5.

Sri Lanka since independence.
See item no. 158.

Sri Lanka in change and crisis.
See item no. 161.

Ceylon: dilemmas of a new nation.
See item no. 165.

**The two wheels of dhamma: essays on the Theravada tradition in India
and Ceylon.**
See item no. 214.

Administration and Local Government

315 **Local government and rural development in Sri Lanka.**
John S. Blackton. Ithaca, New York: Centre for International
Studies, Cornell University. 75p. bibliog.
The interaction between local institutions and the development process in rural
Sri Lanka is the theme of this study, which examines the role of local institutions
with special reference to agricultural productivity, income, local participation and
rural welfare.

316 **Asian bureaucratic systems emergent from the British imperial
tradition.**
Edited by Ralph Braibanti. Durham, North Carolina: Duke
University Press, 1966. 733p.
There are two papers on Sri Lanka in this collection: C. H. Collins' essay on the
imperial heritage examines the structure of the public administration in colonial
Sri Lanka and the ways in which this structure persisted in post-independent Sri
Lanka, and R. N. Kearney's essay on the contemporary bureaucracy discusses the
main features of the bureaucracy and the problems it has faced since
independence.

317 **Regional administration in Sri Lanka.**
Neil Fernando. Colombo: Academy of Administrative Studies,
1973. 69p. bibliog.
The nature of regional administration in Sri Lanka, the processes of change and
the problems it faces in the context of development administration are examined.

318   **A hundred years of local government in Ceylon (1865-1965).**
V. Kanesalingam.   Colombo: Modern Plastic Works, 1971. 198p.
bibliog.

A survey of the role of local government authorities in the administration of the
country since the establishment of the Municipal Councils of Colombo, Galle and
Kandy in 1865.

319   **Local government and decentralized administration in Sri Lanka.**
Tressie G. R. Leitan.   Colombo: Lake House Printers and
Publishers, 1979. 279p. 4 maps. bibliog.

The first such study, this is a detailed account of the functioning of the
government and administration at the district level in Sri Lanka. It explores in
depth the transformation wrought in local government by the appointment of
national politicians to head the district level administration and its implications for
popular participation in administration and for the working out of the centre's
plans for social and economic development at the district level. This is the revised
version of the author's London University PhD thesis.

320   **Kachcheri bureaucracy in Sri Lanka: the culture and politics of
accessibility.**
Namika Raby.   Syracuse, New York: Maxwell School of
Citizenship and Public Affairs, Syracuse University, 1985. 188p.
bibliog. (Foreign and Comparative Studies/South Asian Series, 10).

Focusing on the regional bureaucracy, this anthropological study examines how
the bureaucracy reflects the design of Sri Lankan culture and how the accessibility
to the bureaucracy is shaped and determined by politics and cultural norms and
values. This is the first detailed work on the operation of the regional bureaucracy
in Sri Lanka, and it is based on the author's University of California, San Diego,
doctoral dissertation.

321   **Civil service administration in Ceylon. A study in bureaucratic
adaptation.**
W. A. Wiswa Warnapala.   Colombo: Department of Cultural
Affairs, 1974. 411p. bibliog.

The role and development of the Ceylon Civil Service, in particular the problems
of adaptation it faced in the context of changing political and economic
conditions, are discussed in this study. The emphasis is on the period of the
Donoughmore constitution, 1931-1948. This is the revised version of the author's
Leeds University PhD thesis.

Sri Lanka: a survey.
See item no. 4.

Sinhalese social organization: the Kandyan period.
See item no. 113.

89

Administration and Local Government

Public administration in Ceylon.
See item no. 124.

History of Ceylon from the beginning of the nineteenth century to 1948.
See item no. 129.

Diaries in Ceylon 1908-1911 . . .
See item no. 154.

The politics of Ceylon (Sri Lanka).
See item no. 294.

Politics in Sri Lanka, 1947-1979.
See item no. 312.

A sketch of the constitution of the Kandyan Kingdom and other relevant papers.
See item no. 329.

Constitution and the Legal System

322 **Law and culture in Sri Lanka. A research report on Asian indigenous law.**
Edited by Masaji Chiba.   Tokyo: Research Group on Asian Indigenous Law, 1984. 135p.
This publication reports the preliminary results of the research carried out in Sri Lanka in 1982. The ten essays in the collection address three main themes, methodology and history, official law in interaction with unofficial law, and unofficial law functioning in society. Much of what is offered is not new and the new research is reported in somewhat sketchy fashion. However, the publication is worthy of attention for it embodies the first research initiative in Sri Lanka by the scholars affiliated with the Research Group on Indigenous Law of Japan.

323 **The constitution of 1978.**
Ceylon Journal of Historical and Social Studies, new series, vol. 7, no. 2 (June-Dec. 1977), p. 1-81.
A collection of essays which examine the making of the constitution of 1978, its relationship to the previous constitutions of 1948 and 1972, and its distinctive features.

324 **Sri Lanka: the crisis of the Anglo-American constitutional traditions in a developing society.**
Radhika Coomaraswamy.   New Delhi: Vikas, 1984. 192p. bibliog.
Arguing that ideas and conceptualizations affect political institutions and processes as much as economic interests, the author discusses the 'liberal' constitutional tradition inherited from England and its effectiveness and limitations for Sri Lanka as revealed through the working of the constitutions of 1948, 1972 and 1978.

325 **Constitutional and administrative law of Sri Lanka (Ceylon). A commentary on the constitution and the law of public administration of Sri Lanka.**
Joseph A. L. Cooray. Colombo: Hansa Publishers, 1973. 646p.

A somewhat ponderous but nonetheless useful examination of the constitution of 1972 and administrative law of Sri Lanka. The author's discussion of the making of the 1972 constitution is worthy of attention.

326 **An introduction to the legal system of Ceylon.**
L. J. Mark Cooray. Colombo: Lake House Investments, 1972. 263p. bibliog.

An introductory survey of the systems of laws and the administration of justice in Sri Lanka.

327 **The constitution of the second republic of Sri Lanka (1978) and its significance.**
Chandra Richard de Silva. *Journal of Commonwealth & Comparative Politics*, vol. 17, no. 2 (July 1979), p. 192-209.

The elements of continuity and the novel features in the constitution introduced under the United National Party government in September 1978 are discussed and the significance of the innovations, in particular the presidential system and proportional representation scheme, is evaluated in this essay.

328 **The origins of the law of the Kandyans.**
J. D. M. Derrett. *University of Ceylon Review*, vol. 14, nos. 3-4 (July-Oct. 1956), p. 105-50.

The distinguished legal scholar's contribution to a subject which has long been a puzzlement, the sources of Kandyan law.

329 **A sketch of the constitution of the Kandyan Kingdom and other relevant papers.**
John D'Oyly, edited by L. J. B. Turner. Dehiwala, Sri Lanka: Tisara Prakasakayo, 1975. 241p. map.

This indispensable source for the study of the customary law of the Kandyans and the administration of justice in the Kandyan kingdom is the work of a British official who played a critical role in the defeat of the king of Kandy in 1815 and who, as the principal administrator of the territory, displayed a remarkable sensitivity to the new British subjects. Valuable supplementary material on Kandyan law collected by Simon Sawers, who was the chief judicial officer in Kandy after the conquest, is appended to the work. The first edition of this book appeared in 1929.

330 **Muslim law in Ceylon: an historical outline.**
H. M. Z. Farouque. *Muslim Marriage and Divorce Law Reports*,
vol. 4 (1972), p. 1-28.
An historical survey of Muslim law up to 1948, with emphasis placed on the
statutory changes which took place under British rule.

331 **A treatise on the laws and customs of the Sinhalese, including the
portions still surviving under the name Kandyan law, with
appendices containing Simon Sawers' memoranda, notes on early
decisions, examples of early deeds, etc.**
Fredrick Austin Haley. Colombo: H. W. Cave, 1923. 677p.
The classic work on Sinhalese laws and customs, with extended discussions on the
constitution, administration of justice, crime and punishment, status and social
organization, law of property, intestate succession, contracts, torts and
ecclesiastical law. Yet to be superseded, this work is indispensable to the student
of law but the reader should be aware that Sinhalese laws and customs have been
conceptualized along Western lines, as the organization of the topics testify.

332 **Notes on the constitutional law of colonial Ceylon.**
William Ivor Jennings. *Journal of the Ceylon Branch of the Royal
Asiatic Society*, new series, vol. 1 (1950), p. 51-72.
A valuable commentary on the constitutional law of the British period to which is
appended a list of constitutional documents, 1796-1931.

333 **The constitution of Ceylon.**
William Ivor Jennings. Bombay, India: Oxford University
Press, 1953. 3rd ed. 294p.
The standard work on the constitution of 1948 which was in force until May 1972.
The author was the constitutional adviser to the Sri Lankan leaders who
negotiated the granting of independence from the British in 1948.

334 **The dominion of Ceylon: the development of its laws and
constitution.**
William Ivor Jennings, Henry Wijayakone Tambiah. Westport,
Connecticut: Greenwood Press, 1970. 319p. bibliog.
The three parts of this study examine in detail public law, courts of law and
criminal and civil law respectively. Constitutional and legal changes since 1952,
when the study was originally published, have made it out of date but it is still
valuable for the understanding of Sri Lanka's constitutional and legal structures as
they stood in the immediate post-independence years.

335　Ceylon – a conflict of constitutions.
　　　M. Lakshman Marasinghe. *International and Comparative Law Quarterly*, vol. 20, no. 4 (Oct. 1971), p. 645-74.
A legal scholar's analysis of the process by which the United Front government initiated the introduction of a new Republican constitution.

336　Emergency powers in Sri Lanka, 1817-1959.
　　　Joseph Minattur. *Journal of the Indian Law Institute*, vol. 24, no. 1 (Jan.-March 1982), p. 57-83.
Traces the changes in the form and the nature of use of 'emergency powers', the extraordinary powers possessed by the state to deal with crisis situations. Emphasis is placed on independent Sri Lanka and the perspective adopted is that of a legal scholar.

337　The legal system of Ceylon in its historical setting.
　　　Tambyah Nadaraja.　Leiden, the Netherlands: Brill, 1972. 311p. map. bibliog.
A study of the development of the structure of the judicature and the laws under the Dutch (1656-1796), British (1796-1948), and in independent Sri Lanka. While the text surveys the broad developments, the footnotes embody rich and valuable material and, in fact, the footnotes need to be closely read to make the best use of this work.

338　The legislatures of Ceylon, 1928-1948.
　　　Sagarajasingham Namasivayam.　London: Faber, 1951. 185p. (Studies in Colonial Legislatures, vol. 5).
An examination of the evolution of the colonial legislature, with particular attention devoted to the State Council established under the Donoughmore constitution in 1931.

339　Law and the marriage relationship in Sri Lanka.
　　　Shirani Ponnambalam.　Colombo: Ceylon Printers, 1982. 508p.
Aimed primarily at the legal scholar and practitioner, this study focuses on the law relating to the marital relationship, with detailed discussions on the historical sources of the law and on the principles and rules which have been derived from the personal law systems of Sri Lanka and from Roman-Dutch and English law.

340　The laws and customs of the Tamils of Jaffna.
　　　Henry Wijayakone Tambiah.　Colombo: Times of Ceylon, 1951. 339p.
The standard work on the laws and customs of the Tamils. Special attention has been paid to the *Tēsavalamai*, the codified version of the customary law of the Tamils.

341 **Sinhalese laws and customs.**
Henry Wijayakone Tambiah. Colombo: Lake House
Investments, 1968. 356p.

A general study of the principles of Kandyan law. Though useful, this work lacks authoritative status.

342 **Principles of Ceylon law.**
Henry Wijayakone Tambiah. Colombo: H. W. Cave, 1972. 571p.

An introduction to the laws of Sri Lanka, with attention drawn to both statutory and case law.

343 **The institutes of the laws of Ceylon.**
Henry Byerlay Thomson. London: Trubner, 1866. 2 vols.

This work, by a justice of the Supreme Court, is noteworthy as the first major systematic presentation of the laws of Sri Lanka. It had authoritative status and played an important role in the shaping of the law in colonial times.

344 **The ideology of popular justice in Sri Lanka: a socio-legal inquiry.**
Neelan Tiruchelvam. Delhi: Vikas, 1984. 215p. bibliog.

The significance of popular tribunals in pre-colonial Sri Lanka and the attempts to create popular tribunals in independent Sri Lanka form the focus of this study. Its discussion on the competing conceptions of popular tribunals among policy-makers and the tensions that arose between the traditional institutional form and the socialist goals and aspirations of the new tribunals is penetrating and offers the framework for the understandings of the ultimate failure of these institutions.

345 **The new constitution of Sri Lanka.**
W. A. Wiswa Warnapala. *Asian Survey*, vol. 13, no. 12 (Dec. 1973), p. 1,179-92

An examination of the evolution and the main features of the first autochthonous constitution of Sri Lanka inaugurated in May 1972.

346 **Government and politics in Ceylon, 1931-1946.**
I. D. S. Weerawardana. Colombo: Ceylon Economic Research
Association, 1951. 207p. bibliog.

The standard account of the working of the Donoughmore constitution, which granted universal suffrage.

347 **The Gaullist system in Asia: the constitution of Sri Lanka (1978).**
Alfred Jeyaratnam Wilson. London: Macmillan, 1980. 218p.
bibliog.

The making of the constitution of 1978 is examined in detail. The author discusses the continuities between the new constitution and the previous constitutions of 1972 and 1948 as well as its innovations, the chief of which is the concept of an executive president which is borrowed from Gaullist constitutional thought.

Sri Lanka: a survey.
See item no. 4.

Sinhalese social organization: the Kandyan period.
See item no. 113.

History of Ceylon from the beginning of the nineteenth century to 1948.
See item no. 129.

British Justice and the 'Oriental peasantry': the working of the colonial legal system in nineteenth century Sri Lanka.
See item no. 152.

The people's rights; documents of the Civil Rights Movement of Sri Lanka, 1971 to 1978.
See item no. 157.

Sri Lanka in change and crisis.
See item no. 161.

Universal franchise, 1931-1981: the Sri Lankan experience.
See item no. 286.

Sri Lanka: third world democracy.
See item no. 292.

Politics in Sri Lanka, 1947-1979.
See item no. 312.

Public corporations in Ceylon.
See item no. 394.

Law and social change. A study of land reform in Sri Lanka.
See item no. 411.

Land tenure in village Ceylon: a sociological and historical study.
See item no. 413.

Industrial law and adjudication.
See item no. 445.

The legal framework of industrial relations in Ceylon.
See item no. 446.

An index to periodical articles on the laws of Ceylon.
See item no. 628.

Foreign Relations

348 **Sri Lanka from Dominion to Republic. A study of the changing
relations with the United Kingdom.**
Lucy M. Jacob.   New Delhi: National Publishing House, 1973.
247p. bibliog.
This is a detailed examination of Sri Lanka's relations with the United Kingdom
during the period 1947 to 1972. The emphasis is on political relations; economic
and cultural relations receive less attention. This study is based on a doctoral
dissertation submitted to the University of Rajasthan.

349 **Indo-Ceylon relations since independence.**
Shelton Upatissa Kodikara.   Colombo: Ceylon Institute of World
Affairs, 1965. 262p. bibliog.
Studies the Sri Lankan legislation which was enacted in the immediate post-
independence years to disenfranchise the Indian Tamil plantation workers and the
impact it had on Indo-Sri Lanka relations. The various efforts made by the two
governments to resolve the status of the disenfranchised are also detailed. This is
the revised version of the author's London University doctoral dissertation.

350 **Foreign policy of Sri Lanka: a Third World perspective.**
Shelton Upatissa Kodikara.   Delhi: Chanakya Publications, 1982.
224p.
Examines in turn Sri Lanka's relations with India, the Communist Bloc and the
West.

351 **Sri Lanka's foreign policy: a study in non-alignment.**
H. S. S. Nissanka.   New Delhi: Vikas, 1984. 401p. bibliog.
The emergence of the concept of non-alignment in Sri Lanka's foreign policy, the
foreign policy decision-making process, the country's responses to world crises, its

97

voting behaviour at the United Nations, and the world Non-Aligned Movement summit meeting which was held in Sri Lanka in 1976 are discussed in detail. An epilogue covers the developments since 1977 when the J. R. Jayewardene government came to power, but the author fails to adequately discuss the important changes which have taken place in foreign policy since then and their meaning for the continuity in the non-aligned policy which he charts for the previous period.

352   **Ceylon's foreign policy under the Bandaranaikes (1956-1965). A political analysis.**
Dhirendra Mohan Prasad.   New Delhi: S. Chand, 1973. 465p. bibliog.

A detailed examination of the foreign policies of the Bandaranaikes, emphasizing their commitment to non-alignment. This study is based on the author's Bhagalpur University PhD thesis.

353   **From regionalism to globalism: the role of non-alignment in Sri Lanka's foreign policy.**
Vijaya Samaraweera.   *Asia Quarterly*, no. 4 (1978), p. 277-94.

This essay examines the evolution of Sri Lanka's non-alignment policy in the context of its two principal dimensions, its pragmatic worth in relation to domestic pressures and the demands of geopolitics and its ideological emphasis in relation to the political thinking of the governing political parties.

Sri Lanka: a survey.
See item no. 4.

Sri Lanka since independence.
See item no. 158.

Symposium on Sri Lanka.
See item no. 164.

Politics in Sri Lanka, 1947-1979.
See item no. 312.

Economy

General

354 **Sri Lanka fishermen: rural capitalism and peasant society.**
Paul Alexander.   Canberra: Australian National University Press,
1982. 328p. bibliog. (ANU Monographs on South Asia, no. 7).
A social anthropologist's detailed examination of the economy of beach seine
fishermen in southern Sri Lanka. The author traces the inequalities among the
fishing communities to the impact of capitalist relations of production on the
traditional semi-subsistence economy of the fishermen. This book is based on a
PhD dissertation submitted to the Australian National University.

355 **Economic and social development of Ceylon, 1926-1954.**
Ceylon. Ministry of Finance.   Colombo: Government Press, 1955.
142p.
Surveys economic and social developments and government policies.

356 **The instability of an export economy.**
Gamini Corea.   Colombo: Marga Institute, 1975. 374p. bibliog.
A detailed examination of Sri Lanka's economy between 1930 and 1950 devoted
to the understanding of the role played by fiscal policy in resolving problems faced
by an economy vulnerable to external forces. Three case studies are offered by
way of exemplification: the depression of the 1930s, the Second World War
period, and the post-war boom. This study was originally submitted to Oxford
University as a doctoral dissertation.

357 **A short economic survey of Ceylon.**
B. B. Das Gupta.   Colombo: Associated Newspapers of Ceylon, 1949. 94p. bibliog.

A useful survey of economic developments in the immediate pre-independence period.

358 **Participatory development and dependence – the case of Sri Lanka.**
Godfrey Gunatilleke.   *Marga*, vol. 5, no. 3 (1978), p. 38-174.

This paper, by a noted scholar on development issues, presents the broad social and economic changes that have taken place in Sri Lanka since independence, with the changes themselves being examined in terms of indicators which help to measure the material well-being of the peoples. Useful statistical data is appended.

359 **The economic development of Ceylon. Report of a mission organized by the International Bank for Reconstruction and Development at the request of the government of Ceylon.**
International Bank for Reconstruction and Development.
Baltimore, Maryland: Johns Hopkins Press; London: Oxford University Press, 1953. 529p. 24 maps.

This report, written by a team led by the economist Sir Sydney Caine, provides a comprehensive treatment of Sri Lanka's development issues as they stood in the early 1950s. The report is in two parts. Part one surveys the basic economic development problems and part two analyses in detail problems in specific fields, including trade, monetary policy, rural development, agriculture and coloniz-ation, irrigation, power, industry, transportation, public health, education and technology.

360 **Matching employment opportunities and expectations: a programme of action for Ceylon – the report of an inter-agency team organised by the International Labour Office.**
International Labour Office.   Geneva: International Labour Office, 1971. 2 vols.

The first volume contains the report of the inter-agency team and the second volume the technical papers which formed the basis of the recommendations which were submitted by the team to the government of Sri Lanka. The recommendations called for major reforms in a wide-range of areas, including policy on technology, agriculture, industry, education and exports. The report and the technical papers present a wealth of data but the recommendations proved to be fundamentally flawed in that the drafters clearly failed to recognize the political reality of the circumstances they investigated.

361 **The economy of Ceylon.**
William Ivor Jennings. Madras, India; London: Oxford
University Press, 1951. 2nd ed. 194p.
The standard work on the Sri Lankan economy as it stood at the time of
independence in 1948.

362 **Population growth and economic development in Ceylon.**
Gavin W. Jones, S. Selvaratnam. Colombo: Hansa Publishers in
association with Marga Institute, 1972. 249p.
A comprehensive examination of the implications of alternative population trends
on government expenditure for social welfare, health, education, rice subsidy,
public transport and on the employment and foreign exchange problems. The text
is supplemented by extensive statistical data.

363 **Economic development in Ceylon.**
Halwalage Neville Sepala Karunatilake. New York: Praeger;
London: Pall Mall Press, 1971. 379p. bibliog. (Praeger Special
Studies in International Economics and Development).
This general survey of economic development in Sri Lanka since independence
examines economic policy and development plans, policies on agriculture,
cooperatives, financial institutions, manpower resources and industrialization,
foreign aid and the institutional framework for planning and plan implementation.
The 1960s receive greater attention, and the author highlights the difficulties Sri
Lanka experienced in achieving a high rate of economic growth in the face of
commitment to high level consumption expenditures.

364 **The co-operative system and rural credit in Sri Lanka. A study
undertaken by the Marga Institute for USAID.**
Marga Institute. Colombo: Marga Institute, 1974. 174p. (Marga
Research Studies – 3).
A survey of rural credit needs and the role of state-sponsored cooperatives in
fulfilling them.

365 **Youth, land and employment.**
Marga Institute. Colombo: Marga Institute, 1974. 185p. (Marga
Seminar Papers – 1).
A collection of papers on youth employment opportunities on the land, a subject
which has attracted considerable attention from the state, the public and
academics in contemporary Sri Lanka.

366 **Economic opinion and policy in Ceylon.**
Henry Madison Oliver, Jr. Durham, North Carolina: Duke
University Press; Cambridge, England: Cambridge University
Press, 1957. 145p. bibliog. (Duke University Commonwealth
Studies Center Publications – 6).

This study, covering the period 1916 to 1956, is most impressive in its discussion
of economic opinion, for not only the views of the political leadership but also the
views expressed in academic and popular writings are considered. Its analysis of
economic policy is decidedly less successful, especially with respect to the attempt
to delineate a 'Ceylonese' development theory.

367 **Basic needs, poverty and government policies in Sri Lanka.**
Peter Richards, Wilbert Gooneratne. Geneva: International
Labour Organization, 1980. 176p.

Examines Sri Lanka's welfare policies and its slow rate of growth and high
unemployment and argues against a trade-off between welfare and growth,
positing that the explanation for Sri Lanka's performance is to be found in factors
peculiar to the country and not in the fact that welfare and growth are inherently
incompatible. The study discusses welfare levels, income distribution and poverty,
structural features and structural changes, and policies respectively on the rural
sector, participation in governance, and on education and health.

368 **Employment and unemployment in Ceylon.**
P. J. Richards. Paris: Development Centre, OECD, 1971. 211p.
bibliog. (Development Centre Studies, Employment Series, no. 3).

A policy-oriented study of issues in employment and unemployment in Sri Lanka,
including data from 1953 to 1971. Demographic changes, the labour force and the
labour market, land, labour and agriculture, education and training in
employment, and regional policies are discussed in detail.

369 **Ceylon: an export economy in transition.**
Donald R. Snodgrass. Homewood, Illinois: Richard D. Irwin,
1966. 416p. bibliog.

Characterizing Sri Lanka as an export economy, this study discusses the evolution
of its plantation agriculture sector from its origins in the 1840s. The key to this
analysis is the structuring of the plantations as enclaves, distinct and separate
from peasant agriculture – this dichotomy is identified as the distinguishing mark
of a dual economy. The 1940s are described as the period of revolt against the
export economy and the attempts to reorient the economy through comprehensive economic development are examined in detail. The author's analytic
framework has been questioned in the later literature but the study has not lost its
importance as a major work on the economy of Sri Lanka. The lengthy statistical
appendix is especially valuable.

370 Current economic position and prospects for Ceylon.
South Asia Department, International Bank for Reconstruction and Development. Washington, DC: International Bank for Reconstruction and Development, 1970. 2 vols.

These two volumes present the report of a Bank mission to Sri Lanka. Volume one contains the main report and covers the country's recent economic developments and performance, with in-depth analysis of achievements, problems and prospects in the fields of agriculture and industry. The statistical appendixes to the main report are to be found in volume two.

371 Ceylon.
Stanley Jeyaraj Tambiah. In: *The role of savings and wealth in Southern Asia and the West.* Edited by Richard D. Lambert, Bert F. Hoselitz. Paris: UNESCO, 1963, p. 44-125.

An important essay on the strategies for savings and investment among the different segments in Sri Lankan society, with a particular focus on the critical role played by factors such as religious beliefs in their economic behaviour.

372 Economic implications of population growth. Sri Lanka labour force, 1946-1981.
Pitiyage Wilson. Canberra: Australian National University, 1975. 240p. bibliog.

A comprehensive study of Sri Lanka's labour force, its determining factors, trends, and projections for the decade of 1971-1981.

Sri Lanka: a survey.
See item no. 4.

Sri Lanka: a handbook of historical statistics.
See item no. 74.

History of Ceylon from the beginning of the nineteenth century to 1948.
See item no. 129.

Influence of foreign trade on the level and growth of national income of Ceylon, 1926-57.
See item no. 405.

Development planning

373 **Economic planning, the Green Revolution and 'Food Drive' in Ceylon.**
Gamini Corea. In: *Public finance, planning, and economic development: essays in honour of Ursula Hicks.* Edited by Wilfred L. David. London: Macmillan, 1973, p. 273-303.
An insightful essay by a major figure involved in the planning of the 'Food Drive' initiated by the United National Party government after 1965 with the goal of achieving self-sufficiency in rice and other food crops.

374 **A review of planning for paddy production in Sri Lanka, 1947-70.**
Jayaweera Mudiyanselage Gunadasa. *Modern Ceylon Studies*, vol. 3, no. 2 (July 1972), p. 159-93.
A critical review of policies devoted to increasing paddy production in post-independent Sri Lanka.

375 **Papers by visiting economists.**
J. R. Hicks, Nicholas Kaldor, Joan Robinson, Oskar Lange, John Kenneth Galbraith, Ursula K. Hicks, Gunnar Myrdal. Colombo: Planning Secretariat, 1959. 123p.
This volume brings together papers on issues in the planning and economic development of Sri Lanka written by a group of distinguished economists who were invited by the government of Sri Lanka to advise its National Planning Council. The collection has particular historical value, not only because it highlights the development issues Sri Lanka was facing in the 1950s, but also because it reveals the dominant thinking in the West on the subject of development in the Third World.

376 **Dismantling welfarism in Sri Lanka.**
Janice Jiggins. *ODI Review*, no. 2 (1976), p. 84-104.
A useful overview of development policies in Sri Lanka beewen 1965 and 1976 examined in the context of the welfarism versus growth debate.

377 **Development planning techniques in Sri Lanka.**
Nihal Kappagoda. *Economic Bulletin for Asia and the Pacific*, vol. 25, nos. 2-3 (Sept.-Dec. 1974), p. 89-101.
The evolution of the processes of development planning in Sri Lanka since 1953 and the structural organization that has come into being are discussed.

378 **Welfare and growth in Sri Lanka: a case study of Sri Lanka prepared for the UNRISD project 'the unified approach to development planning & analysis'.**
Marga Institute. Colombo: Marga Institute, 1974. 130p. (Marga Research Studies – 2).

The focus of this study, completed in 1972, is on identifying the critical factors in national development policy and planning experience and their meaning for a unified approach to development planning and analysis. There is a useful statistical appendix.

379 **Local planning within the framework of overall national planning in Sri Lanka.**
Marga Institute. Colombo: Marga Institute, 1976. 69p.

This study undertaken by the Marga Institute on behalf of the Food and Agricultural Organization examines and evaluates Sri Lanka's planning and administration in relation to the participation of local level entities and organizations in the planning process.

380 **The planning implications of the Mahaweli Development Project in Sri Lanka.**
M. W. J. G. Mendis. Colombo: Lake House Investments, 1973. 154p. bibliog.

Adopting an integrated approach to planning, the author critically examines the spatial and social implications of the recommendations for village settlements put forward by the UNDP/FAO mission which reported to the government of Sri Lanka on the Mahavali project. This is the published version of the author's dissertation submitted for the MSc degree in Urban and Regional Planning at the University of Strathclyde in Scotland.

381 **Employment approaches to economic planning in developing countries, with special reference to the development planning of Ceylon (Sri Lanka).**
Birger Möller. Lund, Sweden: Student litteratur AB, 1972. 305p. map. bibliog. (Scandinavian Institute of Asian Studies Monograph Series, no. 9).

A critical examination of development planning and its implications for the creation of employment opportunities in the period 1948-68.

382 **Economic development in South Asia: proceedings of a conference held by the International Economic Association at Kandy, Ceylon.**
Edited by E. A. G. Robinson, Michael Kidron. London: Macmillan; New York: St. Martin's Press, 1970. 585p.

Includes two papers by Sri Lankan economists: one on the recent approaches to planning in Sri Lanka by L. Jayawardena, and one on choice of techniques in Sri Lanka by B. Hewavitharana.

383 **The state and income distribution, with a case study of Sri Lanka.**
Peter de Valk.   The Hague: Institute of Social Studies, 1981.
159p. bibliog.

A case study of Sri Lanka's development dilemma: responding to political
pressures, successive governments have pursued compensatory public intervention
as the strategy of ensuring basic welfare but the achievements have been wrought
at a high cost, as reflected in the slow rate of growth, high unemployment, and
import costs. The author examines the ground covered in many other recent
studies of development in Sri Lanka but his volume is useful for its succinct
presentation of the issues.

Sri Lanka: a survey.
See item no. 4.

Symposium on Sri Lanka.
See item no. 164.

Finance and Banking

384 Economic policies and their implication for the foreign exchange resource availability in Sri Lanka, 1956-1972.
P. A. S. Dahanayake.   Colombo: Central Bank of Ceylon, 1977.
250p. bibliog. (Central Bank of Ceylon Research Series – 8).
The policies of different governments towards the availability of foreign exchange during a period of foreign exchange difficulty and the constraints foreign exchange availability imposed upon the national economy are examined in this study.

385 Bank behaviour and control of credit flows: lessons from the Sri Lanka experience.
Jamshed K. S. Gandhi, Katrine Anderson Saito.   Washington, DC: Public and Private Finance Division, Development Economics Department, World Bank, 1977. 38p. (Studies in Domestic Finance, no. 41).
Reviews credit control policies and mechanisms of Sri Lanka's banking institutions.

386 From dependent currency to central banking in Ceylon: an analysis of monetary experience 1825-1957.
H. A. de Silva Gunasekera.   London: Bell, 1962. 324p. bibliog.
A comprehensive treatment of policies relating to money and banking, both under British rule and in independent Sri Lanka. This work is based on the author's London University doctoral dissertation.

387 **Banking and financial institutions in Ceylon.**
Halwalage Neville Sepala Karunatilake.   Colombo: Central Bank
of Ceylon, 1968. 270p. bibliog.
A comprehensive analysis of banking and financial developments in Sri Lanka
since independence. The emphasis is on the institutional arrangements.

388 **Central banking and monetary policy in Sri Lanka.**
Halwalage Neville Sepala Karunatilake.   Colombo: Lake House
Investments, 1973. 209p. bibliog.
A historical survey of the Central Bank of Sri Lanka and its operations, with
particular emphasis on its statutory role in monetary policy-making.

389 **Ceylon currency and banking.**
Belikoth Ragunath Shenoy.   London: Longmans, Green, 1941.
300p. bibliog.
This pioneering historical study of the development of money and banking in Sri
Lanka continues to merit attention, especially for developments which took place
in the early period of British rule.

390 **Agricultural credit in a developing economy – Ceylon.**
W. M. Tilakaratna.   Colombo: Central Bank of Ceylon, 1963.
234p. bibliog. (Central Bank of Ceylon Research Series).
The subject of this revised version of the author's London University PhD thesis
is the role of credit in the agricultural sector. Its discussion of the farmers' sources
of credit is particularly valuable.

391 **Banks and banking law in Ceylon.**
Wickrema Sena Weerasooriya.   Colombo: Bankers Training
Institute of Sri Lanka, 1974. 239p. bibliog.
The evolution of the legal framework of the banking industry in Sri Lanka is the
subject of this published version of the author's London University PhD thesis.

392 **Credit and security in Ceylon (Sri Lanka); the legal problems of
development finance.**
Wickrema Sena Weerasooriya, David E. Allen, Mary E. Hiscock,
Derek Roebuck.   St. Lucia, Queensland, Australia: University of
Queensland Press; New York: Crane, Russak, 1973. 303p. bibliog.
(Law and Development Finance in Asia, vol. 4).
A review of the legal framework for private sector credit and the lending policies
of the financing institutions of Sri Lanka.

Trade and Industry

393 Rice and rubber. The story of China-Ceylon trade.
S. P. Amarasingham.   Colombo: Ceylon Economic Research
Association, 1953. 208p. bibliog.
The first major bi-lateral trade agreement of independent Sri Lanka, the exchange
of Sri Lanka's rubber for China's rice, is the subject of this study.

394 Public corporations in Ceylon.
Anthony Ranjith Bevis Amerasinghe.   Colombo: Lake House
Investments, 1971. 349p. bibliog.
The public corporations and their role in national development are the focus of
this study. All the corporations are examined individually, and there is a
particularly useful discussion of their legal framework.

**395 Tourism in Sri Lanka: the mapping of international inequalities and
their internal structural effects.**
Susantha Goonatilake.   Montreal: Centre for Developing Area
Studies, McGill University, 1978. 29p. map. (Working Papers,
no. 19).
The socio-economic impact of the growing tourist industry is examined critically
in this paper.

396 External trade and the economic structure of Ceylon, 1900-55.
Elaine Gunawardena.   Colombo: Central Bank of Ceylon, 1965.
234p. bibliog. (Central Bank of Ceylon Research Series).
A historical study of the development of external trade of Sri Lanka and its
impact on the economy. The text is supplemented by comprehensive statistical
data.

397 **Indo-Ceylon trade and economic relations.**
Buddhadasa Hewavitharana. *Ceylon Historical Journal*, vol. 19, nos. 1-4 (July 1969-April 1970), p. 82-176.

An examination of trade and economic relations between the two neighbouring countries from the mid-1950s when, as the author argues, the new economic, social and political milieus of international trade of the countries impacted upon the traditional patterns.

398 **Pricing policies of public enterprises. A country study of selected public enterprises in Ceylon.**
V. Kanesalingam. Colombo: Documentation and Publications Division, Industrial Development Board of Ceylon, 1972. 128p. bibliog. map.

Though the thrust of the study is somewhat technical, the discussion is not narrow, and valuable information about the working of the public enterprises in Sri Lanka may be obtained from it.

399 **Techno-economic survey of industrial potential in Sri Lanka.**
Neil Dias Karunaratne. Colombo: Industrial Development Board, 1973. 398p. bibliog.

This comprehensive study identifies and evaluates the industrial potential of Sri Lanka from the perspective of an econometrician. The failure of the author to take into account the political dimensions of policy making considerably diminishes the policy recommendations he puts forward.

400 **Political economy of controlling transnationals. Pharmaceutical industry in Sri Lanka.**
Sanjaya Lall, Senaka Bible. *Economic and Political Weekly*, vol. 12, nos. 33-34 (Aug. 1977), p. 1,419-36.

Sri Lanka's experience with manufacturing, importing, and distributing pharmaceuticals to the exclusion of multinational pharmaceutical organizations during the period 1972 to 1976 is reviewed in this paper.

401 **Trade and growth: the case of Ceylon.**
Youngil Lim. *Economic Development and Cultural Change*, vol. 16, no. 2 (Jan. 1968), p. 245-60.

Foreign trade between 1830 and 1961 is examined in order to determine its impact on the growth of Sri Lanka's economy.

402 **Sri Lanka, Third World and UNCTAD IV.**
Marga Institute. *Marga*. vol. 3, no. 2 (1976), p. 1-169.

This special issue of *Marga* is devoted to the examination of the implications of the 4th United Nations Conference on Trade and Development for the Third World in general and Sri Lanka in particular.

403   **Technology-transfer and reverse flow.**
       Marga Institute.   *Marga*, vol. 5, no. 2 (1978), p. 1-118.
Two studies prepared by the Marga Institute for the UNCTAD Secretariat are
presented in this special issue of *Marga*. The first study is on the Sri Lankan
experience relating to the transfer of technology in the manufacturing sector up to
1975, and the second is on the Sri Lankan experience with reverse transfer of
technology. Both studies present valuable data and the discussions focus primarily
on the policy implications of the issues raised.

404   **Report of reconnaissance mission to Ceylon in connection with state
       industrial corporations, Feb. 16th-March 16th, 1966.**
       George W. Naylor.   Colombo: Ministry of Planning and
       Economic Affairs, 1966. 147p. map.
A survey of eighteen state industrial corporations which highlights serious
deficiencies in their organization, location, management, labour relations, and
marketing policies.

405   **Influence of foreign trade on the level and growth of national
       income of Ceylon, 1926-57.**
       Warnasena Rasaputram.   Colombo: Central Bank of Ceylon,
       1964. 187p. bibliog. (Central Bank of Ceylon Research Series).
Adopting the analytical framework of stability and economic growth, the author
examines the impact which both exports and imports had on the growth of
national income during the period. Particular attention is paid to tea and rubber,
Sri Lanka's main exports. This study is based on the author's University of
Wisconsin PhD thesis.

406   **Report of the Commission of Inquiry on Agency Houses and
       Brokering Firms.**
       Sri Lanka.   Commission of Inquiry on Agency Houses and
       Brokering Firms.   Colombo: Department of Government
       Printing, 1974. 641p. (Sessional Paper xii of 1974).
This report of the Presidential Commission provides the most extensive
documentation on the structure and the working of agency houses which
dominated the management of tea, rubber and coconut plantations and the export
of their products since the 19th century. The commission's report is critical of the
agency houses and it recommended government take-over of their main function.

407   **Sri Lanka's gem industry.**
      Economic Review, vol. 3, no. 6 (Sept. 1977), p. 3-15.
An examination of the gem industry in Sri Lanka – in particular since the
establishment of the State Gem Corporation in 1971 – and the importance gem
exports have achieved as a 'non-traditional' source of foreign exchange earnings
for the country.

Trade and Industry

Sri Lanka: a survey.
See item no. 4.

History of Ceylon from the beginning of the nineteenth century to 1948.
See item no. 129.

Industrial Ceylon: a select bibliography.
See item no. 621.

Transport
and Communications

408 History of the Public Works Department, Ceylon 1796-1913.
P. M. Bingham.   Colombo: Government Printer, 1921-23. 3 vols.

Reviews the accomplishments of the department in opening up the country through communication networks, beginning with the establishment of British rule.

409 The Ceylon government railway: one hundred years, 1864-1964.
Ceylon.   Ceylon Government Railway. Colombo: Government Press, 1964. 174p. map.

A celebration and review of the development of the railway system in Sri Lanka.

History of Ceylon from the beginning of the nineteenth century to 1948.
See item no. 129.

Fifty years in Ceylon. An autobiography.
See item no. 153.

Land Tenure
and Land Reform

410 **Ancient land tenure and revenue in Ceylon.**
Humphrey William Codrington. Colombo: Government Printer, 1950. 70p.

The standard work (originally published in 1938) on the system of land tenure and revenue in early Sri Lanka and its evolution to the 1930s, this study remains essential reading, even though some of its conclusions have been contested by recent works.

411 **Law and social change. A study of land reform in Sri Lanka.**
Martin E. Gold. New York, London: Nelson, 1977. 252p.

Adopting the conceptual framework of law and modernization, the author examines the various land reform measures enacted by successive governments from 1958 onwards, devoting particular attention to the politics of land reform, the form of legislation and implementation.

412 **Land tenure problems and land reforms in Ceylon.**
Wilbert Gooneratne. Tokyo: Institute of Developing Economies, 1975. 65p. bibliog. map.

An overview of issues in land tenure and policy responses to them.

413 **Land tenure in village Ceylon: a sociological and historical study.**
Gananath Obeyesekere. Cambridge, England: Cambridge University Press, 1966. 319p. 2 maps. bibliog. (Cambridge South Asian Studies).

The interaction of land tenurial arrangements and social structure as seen from both a historical and a sociological perspective is considered in detail in this influential study. There are extended discussions of the traditional inheritance laws, kinship and marriage, legal changes introduced by the British and the changes which took place in both land holding patterns and social structure as a result of economic development under the British.

414   The current land reforms and peasant agriculture in Sri Lanka.
Gerald H. Peiris.   *South Asia*, no. 5 (Dec. 1975), p. 78-89.

A discussion of the Land Reform Act of 1972 in relation to the changes envisaged in the peasant sector. It argues that in anticipating increases in productivity and employment in peasant agriculture, the reformers ignored the past experience of converting large agricultural landholdings into peasant holdings and the performance of peasant cooperative farms.

415   Share tenancy and tenurial reform in Sri Lanka.
Gerald H. Peiris.   *Ceylon Journal of Historical and Social Studies*, new series, vol. 6, no. 1 (Jan.-June 1976), p. 24-54.

The author presents a valuable synthesis of the literature on the subject of *ande* cultivation, the name by which share tenancy is known in Sri Lanka, and discusses the impact the share tenancy system had on land tenurial reform policy considerations.

416   Land reform and agrarian change in Sri Lanka.
Gerald H. Peiris.   *Modern Asian Studies*, vol. 12, no. 4 (Oct. 1978), p. 611-28.

A useful review of land reform measures and their impact on agrarian change in Sri Lanka culminating with a discussion of the Land Reform Act of 1972 which imposed ceilings on the ownership of land except in the plantation sector.

417   Land reform in Sri Lanka.
Vijaya Samaraweera.   *Third World Legal Studies* (1982), p. 104-22.

The major land reform measures introduced by the United Front government in 1972 and 1975 are discussed and the author argues that the potential the measures had of fundamentally transforming the structure of the agrarian sector was nullified because of the failure to articulate clearly stated goals for the legislation.

418   Sri Lanka's new land reform.
Nimal Sanderatne.   *South Asian Review*, vol. 6, no. 1 (Oct. 1972), p. 7-20.

This essay identifies the Land Reform Act of 1972 as the first attempt to alter the existing property structure in Sri Lanka through the redistribution of land expropriated after the imposition of a ceiling on privately owned land. The exemption of company owned property from the law has meant that the bulk of the holdings which were over the ceiling did not come within government control for redistribution. Further, it is argued, the impact of the law has been considerably weakened by a discretionary element which has enabled some families to maintain large holdings and by a failure to come to grips with problems of tenure of paddy lands.

419   Land tenure and revenue in mediaeval Ceylon (A.D. 1000-1500).
      Wathuge Indrakirti Siriweera.   *Ceylon Journal of Historical and*
      Social Studies, new series, vol. 2, no. 1 (Jan.-June 1972), p. 1-49.
An important contribution to the understanding of land tenure and revenue in
early Sri Lanka. The author argues that land and rights accruing from land were
not structured in a highly centralized system with its locus in the kingship but
rather that the king shared rights with many other institutions and individuals,
thereby revealing a multi-centred and complex pattern of rights and obligations
arising out of land. Similarly, he contends, the revenue administration reflected a
multi-centred socio-economic structure rather than one which was highly
centralized and ordered rigidly.

420   **Policies and implementation of land reform in Sri Lanka – case**
      studies.
      Ranjith D. Wanigaratne, Wilbert Gooneratne,
      N. Shanmugaratnam.   Colombo: Agrarian Research and Training
      Institute, 1978. 81p.
Case studies of three Sinhalese villages focusing on the impact of socio-political
and economic processes on the implementation of land reform measures.

Agrarian policies of the Dutch in South-West Ceylon, 1743-1767.
See item no. 110.

History of Ceylon from the beginning of the nineteenth century to 1948.
See item no. 129.

Population, land and structural change in Sri Lanka and Thailand.
See item no. 168.

Pul Eliya. A village in Ceylon. A study of land tenure and kinship.
See item no. 240.

Report of the Kandyan Peasantry Commission.
See item no. 246.

Agriculture

421 An overview of settlement schemes in Sri Lanka.
Nihal Amerasinghe. *Asian Survey*, vol. 16, no. 7 (July 1976),
p. 620-36.
A survey of both old land settlement schemes, identified as those established
between 1936 and 1966, and the new and the factors which differentiate them.

422 Ceylon agriculture. A perspective.
Puran Chand Bansil. Delhi: Dhanpat Rai & Sons, 1971. 407p.
maps. bibliog.
This work offers the most comprehensive treatment of agriculture in Sri Lanka in
a single volume. Both the peasant sector and plantation agriculture are considered
but greater attention is devoted to peasant agriculture. Useful data is appended to
the discussion.

**423 Understanding green revolutions. Agrarian change and develop-
ment planning in South Asia. Essays in honour of B. H. Farmer.**
Edited by Timothy P. Bayliss-Smith, Sudhir Wanmali.
Cambridge, England: Cambridge University Press, 1984. 384p.
bibliog.
Three essays focus on Sri Lanka's experience with the Green Revolution:
Vidyamali Samamarasinghe and S. W. R. de A. Samarasinghe analyse the income
and wealth disparities in a land settlement colony in the dry zone, C. M.
Madduma Banadara offers a comparative study of water demand for agriculture
in Tamil Nadu and Sri Lanka, and John C. Harriss discusses the ideology,
planning and practice of irrigation in settlement schemes.

424 **Internal structure and organization of the tea industry: an overview.**
Paul Caspersz. *Marga*, vol. 2, no. 4 (1975), p. 38-64.
A survey of the structure and organization of the tea industry examined from the perspective of its role as the principal export of Sri Lanka. Statistical data supplement the text.

425 **Politics and land settlement schemes: the case of Sri Lanka.**
David Dunham. *Development and Change*, vol. 13 (1982), p. 43-61.
Argues that the settlement schemes, ranging from those initiated in the 1930s to those conceived under the Mahavali programme, should be understood not in terms of their stated objectives but rather in terms of the contradictions in Sri Lanka's social structure and the manner in which the ruling class uses the state apparatus to solve the problems arising out of the contradictions. Thus, politics is not a marginal issue but has a central role to play in settlement policies.

426 **New settlement schemes in Sri Lanka. A study of twenty selected youth schemes, co-operative farms, DDC agricultural projects, and land reform settlements.**
Anthony O. Ellman, D. de S. Ratnaweera. Colombo: Agrarian Research and Training Institute, 1974. 234p. (Research Study Series, no. 5).
The four types of land settlement schemes – youth schemes, co-operative farms, District Development Council schemes, and land reform settlements – which were introduced after the adoption of the land reform measure of 1972 under which the state was empowered to acquire privately held land above defined ceilings are examined comparatively in this study.

427 **Land settlement in Sri Lanka 1840-1975. A review of the major writings on the subject.**
Anthony O. Ellman, D. de S. Ratnaweera, K. T. Silva, G. Wickremasinghe. Colombo: Agrarian Research and Training Institute, 1976. 94p. bibliog. (Research Study Series, no. 16).
A valuable guide to the literature on land settlement in Sri Lanka, with an extensive bibliography.

428 **Farm power in Sri Lanka.**
J. Farrington, F. Abeyratne. Reading, England: Department of Agricultural Economics and Management, University of Reading, 1982. 272p. bibliog. map.
Presents the results of a study undertaken on the needs of farm power, human, draught and mechanical.

429 **Pioneer peasant colonization in Ceylon: a study in Asian agriculture.**
Bertram Hughes Farmer. West Hartford, Connecticut:
Greenwood, 1976. 387p. 12 maps. bibliog.
This authoritative study, first published in 1957, provides a geographical introduction to the dry zone, where state-sponsored colonization schemes have been established, a survey of the evolution of the policy on colonization from the British times, and a detailed and critical examination of the immediate pre-independent and post-independent colonization schemes.

430 **Green revolution? Technology and change in rice-growing areas of Tamil Nadu and Sri Lanka.**
Edited by Bertram Hughes Farmer. London: Macmillan;
Boulder, Colorado: Westview, 1977. 429p. 6 maps. bibliog.
Presents the results of the field studies on the impact of the Green Revolution technology on rice-growing carried out by an inter-disciplinary study group. A series of essays examine the Sri Lankan data from a variety of viewpoints. There are also several essays which offer comparative data on Sri Lanka and Tamil Nadu.

431 **Mahaweli Ganga irrigation and hydro-power survey. Final general report.**
Food and Agricultural Organization and Irrigation Department,
Ceylon. Colombo: Project Manager, 1968. 2 parts.
This report embodies the results of the survey conducted in 1963 on the feasibility of developing the resources of the Mahavali Ganga, the largest river in Sri Lanka, for irrigation, land settlement and generation of power. It proved to be the first of the several major reports that were to be issued on the development of the Mahavali basin.

432 **A hundred years of Ceylon tea, 1867-1967.**
Denys Mastyn Forrest. London: Chatto & Windus, 1967. 320p.
map. bibliog.
A highly readable account of the history of the tea industry, with a particularly evocative description of its early stages and the pioneer entrepreneurs.

433 **Rice revolution in Sri Lanka.**
N. D. Abdul Hameed, Nihal Amerasinghe, Bernard Leslie
Panditharatne, G. D. A. Gunasekera, Joseph Selvadurai,
Somasundaram Selvanayagam. Geneva: UN Research Institute
for Social Development, 1977. 282p. (Report No. 76.7; Studies on
the Green Revolution, no. 13).
A detailed examination of the state policy devoted to the improvement of the productivity of paddy cultivation in Sri Lanka, with particular attention given to the impact of the introduction of high-yielding varieties of rice. Four case studies from different regions of the country form the core of the work.

434 **Some aspects of the tea industry.**
Nalini Jeyapalan, A. S. Jayawardena. *Central Bank of Ceylon
Bulletin*, vol. 17, no. 6 (June 1967), p. 16-27; vol. 17, no. 8 (Aug.
1967), p. 23-42; vol. 17, no. 10 (Oct. 1967), p. 23-39; vol. 18, no. 3
(March 1968), p. 19-63.
A general survey of Sri Lanka's tea industry and an excellent analysis of factors
affecting the tea export trade.

435 **Tea in Ceylon. An attempt at a regional and temporal
differentiation of the tea growing areas in Ceylon.**
Heidrun Marby. Wiesbaden, GFR: Franz Steiner, 1972. 238p.
18 maps. bibliog. (Geoecological Research, vol. I).
A study of the ecology of the tea growing areas, the central highlands and
foothills of the South West, through a focus on the tea plant and its interaction
with the environment into which it was introduced.

436 **The management of irrigation systems in Sri Lanka: a study in
practical sociology.**
M. P. Moore. *Sri Lanka Journal of Social Sciences*, vol. 2, no. 2
(Dec. 1979), p. 89-112.
An excellent review of various measures developed – some experimentally – for
the design and operation of irrigation systems and for institutions of water
management by the Sri Lanka government and its agencies.

437 **The effect of price fluctuations on rubber productions in Ceylon: a
study of the Great Depression and the Korean War Boom.**
Gerald H. Peiris. *Ceylon Journal of Historical and Social Studies*,
new series, vol. 2, no. 1 (Jan.-June 1972), p. 75-87.
This essay is an examination of the ways in which different segments of Sri
Lanka's rubber industry – company estates, privately-owned large holdings, and
small-holdings – responded to the diametrically different price fluctuations in
natural rubber which took place during two crucial periods, the Great Depression
of the early 1930s and the Korean War Boom of the early 1950s.

438 **Reflections on agrarian research in Sri Lanka in the 1970s.**
Gerald H. Peiris. *Ceylon Journal of Historical and Social Studies*,
new series, vol. 6, no. 2 (July-Dec. 1976), p. 48-68.
A critical review of agrarian research in the 1970s to which is appended a useful
annotated bibliography of over 130 publications, including mimeographed
material issued by such agencies as the Agrarian Research and Training Institute,
Agricultural Diversification Project of the United Nations Development
Fund/Food and Agriculture Organization, Department of Agriculture, and the
Mahavali Development Board.

439 **Proceedings of a symposium on 'The Development of Agriculture in the Dry Zone'.**
Edited by O. S. Peries.   Colombo: Ceylon Association for the Advancement of Science, 1968. 236p. bibliog.

A collection of uneven papers on the principles of land utilization, soil and water problems, research problems, problems of agricultural development and economics. A select bibliography on the development of agriculture in the dry zone is appended.

440 **Plantation rubber industry in Ceylon.**
S. Rajaratnam.   *University of Ceylon Review*, vol. 20, no. 1 (Apr. 1962), p. 96-124

Surveys the emergence and the early development of the rubber industry, from 1886 to 1931.

441 **Foreign plantation investment in Ceylon.**
N. Ramachandran.   Colombo: Central Bank of Ceylon, 1963. 200p. bibliog. (Central Bank of Ceylon Research Series).

The financial experience of the sterling tea and rubber companies which operated in Sri Lanka between 1889 and 1958 is detailed in this study on the basis of research on a random sample. The formation of companies, their methods of raising capital, investment strategies, effects of taxation, and the gradual transfer of ownership from foreign to Sri Lankan hands are the major topics examined.

442 **Agriculture in Ceylon until 1975.**
Peter Richards, E. Stoutjesdik.   Paris: Development Centre of the Organization for Economic Co-operation and Development, 1970. 228p. bibliog. (Development Centre Studies).

A policy-oriented study which examines the factors which need to be taken into account in the formulation of an agricultural policy which has as its goal self-sufficiency in food production.

443 **Agriculture in the peasant sector of Sri Lanka.**
Edited by S. W. R. de A. Samarasinghe.   Peradeniya, Sri Lanka: Ceylon Studies Seminar, 1977. 302p.

In this collection of thirteen papers, specialists in the respective fields examine a variety of issues in peasant agriculture, ranging from water resources to rural credit and marketing. The focus is primarily on the institutional aspects.

444 **Field crops of Ceylon.**
S. T. Senewiratne, R. R. Appadurai.   Colombo: Lake House Investments, 1966. 376p.

A handbook of the main field crops of Sri Lanka.

Agriculture

Sri Lanka: a survey.
See item no,. 4.

The agroclimate of Ceylon. A contribution towards the ecology of tropical crops.
See item no. 18.

Golden tips. A description of Ceylon and its great tea industry.
See item no. 36.

History of Ceylon from the beginning of the nineteenth century to 1948.
See item no. 129.

Economic planning, the Green Revolution and 'Food Drive' in Ceylon.
See item no. 373.

A bibliography of socio-economic studies in the agrarian sector of Sri Lanka.
See item no. 631.

122

Labour Relations, Labour Movements and Trade Unions

445 Industrial law and adjudication.
W. E. M. Abeyesekera. Colombo: Colombo Apothecaries, 1970. 4 vols.

A practising lawyer's comprehensive examination of the statutory and case law relating to industrial relations.

446 The legal framework of industrial relations in Ceylon.
Sriyan Ranjith de Silva. Colombo: H. W. Cave, 1973. 679p.

A detailed study of the legal framework of industrial relations, emphasizing the significance of the role of the state. The author also offers a critical analysis of the statutory provisions and the case law.

447 Some concepts of labour law.
Sriyan Ranjith de Silva. Colombo: Lake House Investments, 1977. 196p.

Concepts of equity, gratuity, employer-employee relations, and termination of employment are analysed within the framework of international labour relations and Sri Lankan case law.

448 Industrial democracy, co-determination and worker participation in Sri Lanka.
Sriyan Ranjith de Silva. Colombo: Co-determination Project, Asian Council for Law in Development, 1978. 40p.

This paper examines the various forms of worker participation in the industrial relations context and assesses the feasibility of introducing co-determination into Sri Lanka.

449   **The rise of the labor movement in Ceylon.**
Visakha Kumari Jayawardena.   Durham, North Carolina: Duke
University Press, 1972. 382p. bibliog.

An account of the emergence of the labour movement in Sri Lanka during the
period 1880 to 1933. The first part details the interweaving of the incipient labour
movement with the religious revivalism of the late 19th and early 20th centuries
and the early nationalist movement, and the second part traces the relationship
between nationalist politics and the labour movement. In the latter discussion,
particular attention is devoted to the career of the pioneer trade unionist, A. E.
Goonasinha, who receives less than critical attention.

450   **Trade unions and politics in Ceylon.**
Robert N. Kearney.   Berkeley, California; Los Angeles; London:
University of California Press, 1971. 195p. bibliog.

A pioneering study of trade unions in Sri Lanka, their role in industrial relations
and, in particular, their impact upon the political process.

Education

451 **Education in Ceylon (from the sixth century B.C. to the present day). A centenary volume.**
Ceylon. Ministry of Education and Cultural Affairs. Colombo: Government Press, 1969. 3 vols. bibliog.
Issued to mark the centenary of the establishment of the Department of Public Instruction by the British in 1869, this volume is a collective attempt to chart the developments in education in Sri Lanka from the earliest times. The coverage is broad – thus, not only secondary and higher education but also libraries and museums are examined – but the essays are of uneven quality. A comprehensive bibliography is included.

452 **Final report of the National Education Commission.**
Ceylon. National Education Commission. Colombo: Government Press, 1962. 241p. (Sessional Paper vii of 1962).
This report made a comprehensive review of the system of education then existing and presented major recommendations for reforms which were to greatly influence the government's formulation of educational policy over the next decade and a half.

453 **One hundred years of education in Ceylon.**
J. C. A. Corea. *Modern Asian Studies*, vol. 3, no. 2 (April 1969), p. 151-75.
A sweeping survey of educational developments in Sri Lanka since the establishment of the Department of Public Instruction by the British in 1869.

454 **Weightage in university admissions. Standardization and district quotas in Sri Lanka.**
Chandra Richard de Silva. *Modern Ceylon Studies*, vol. 5, no. 2 (July 1974), p. 152-78.

A superb analysis of the innovation in university admission policy which brought about bitter resentment among the Tamil youth who were shut out from the universities. This policy arguably contributed to the deterioration of the relations between the Sinhalese and Tamils.

455 **The politics of university admissions: a review of some aspects of the admissions policy in Sri Lanka, 1971-1978.**
Chandra Richard de Silva. *Sri Lanka Journal of Social Sciences*, vol. 1, no. 2 (Dec. 1978), p. 85-123.

Analyses key issues in higher education in the 1970s, in particular the standardization scheme and the district quota system introduced by the government for university admissions in response to pressure exerted by sectional interests. Of particular value is the discussion on the critical importance of the university admissions issue for Sinhalese-Tamil relations and the changes that took place in the ethnic composition of those who were successful in gaining entry into the universities. The latter discussion is supplemented by statistical data from official sources published here for the first time.

456 **The universities and the government in Sri Lanka.**
Kingsley Muthumuni de Silva. *Minerva*, vol. 16, no. 2 (Summer 1978), p. 251-72.

The role the government has played since 1921 in higher education in Sri Lanka is considered in this essay within the context of an issue which assumed heightened importance beginning from the 1960s, the autonomous status of the universities.

457 **Education in Sri Lanka under the Portuguese.**
W. L. A. Don Peter. Colombo: Colombo Catholic Press, 1978. 342p. map. bibliog.

A comprehensive treatment of education during Portuguese rule. Of particular value is the author's examination of the role education played in Catholic missionary activities.

458 **Financing and educational policy in Sri Lanka (Ceylon).**
Jacques Hallak. Paris: UNESCO International Institute for Educational Planning, 1972. 159p. bibliog. (Financing Educational Systems: Country Case Studies, no. 1).

An analysis of the educational policies of the 1960s and the cost of financing education in the 1970s, together with a consideration of the role played by socio-economic factors in the formulation of educational policy in Sri Lanka.

459　**Developments in university education: the growth of the University of Ceylon (1942-1965).**
D. Laksiri Jayasuriya. *University of Ceylon Review*, vol. 23, nos. 1-2 (April-Oct. 1965), p. 83-153.
A useful review, with statistical data, of higher education in Sri Lanka from the establishment of the University of Ceylon.

460　**Education in Ceylon before and after independence, 1939-1968.**
John Ernest Jayasuriya. Colombo: Associated Educational Publishers, 1969. 318p.
A critical survey of developments and achievements in education by a prominent educator.

461　**Educational policies and progress during British rule in Ceylon (Sri Lanka) 1796-1948.**
John Ernest Jayasuriya. Colombo: Associated Educational Publishers, 1976. 558p. bibliog.
Examines in great detail the educational policies of the British and their impact on social progress in colonial Sri Lanka.

462　**Educational expansion and political volatility in Sri Lanka: the 1971 insurrection.**
Robert N. Kearney. *Asian Survey*, vol. 15, no. 9 (Sept. 1975), p. 727-44.
Studies the links between the expansion of educational opportunities, the thwarted employment expectations of the educated youth, and the successful recruitment of the disaffected youth by the Janatha Vimukti Peramuna whose activities culminated in the April 1971 Insurrection.

463　**Non-formal education in Sri Lanka. A study undertaken by the Marga Institute for the International Council for Educational Development and United Nations Children's Fund.**
Marga Institute. Colombo: Marga Institute, 1974. 242p. (Marga Research Studies – 1).
The most informative account available of the non-governmental institutions and agencies which provide educational services, in particular in the rural areas.

464　**Schools for a new nation: the development and administration of the educational system of Ceylon.**
Wallace R. Muelder. Colombo: K. V. G. de Silva, 1962. 216p. bibliog.
An examination of Sri Lanka's educational system which notes its strengths and weaknesses from the standpoint of both financial and organizational considerations.

465 **Universities, politics and public opinion in Ceylon.**
Ralph Pieris. *Minerva* (Summer 1954), p. 435-54.
This searching inquiry into the interaction between higher education and politics
is still worthy of attention.

466 **University admissions in Ceylon: their economic and social
background and employment expectations.**
G. Uswatte-Aratchi. *Modern Asian Studies*, vol. 8, no. 3 (July
1974), p. 289-318.
The persons who had access to university education, their employment expectations and the changes to be found in the spread of higher educational
opportunities between 1950 and 1967 are examined in this essay.

467 **Sri Lanka – non-formal education for rural youth.**
Edward L. Wijemanne, G. H. F. Welikala. In: *Education for
rural development: case studies for planners*. Edited by Manzoor
Ahamed, Philip H. Coombs. New York: Praeger, 1975,
p. 249-92.
The condensed version of the case study on *Non-formal education in Sri
Lanka* . . . (q.v.) conducted by the Marga Institute.

Sri Lanka: a survey.
See item no. 4.

Modern Sri Lanka: a society in transition.
See item no. 5.

History of Ceylon from the beginning of the nineteenth century to 1948.
See item no. 129.

Symposium on Sri Lanka.
See item no. 164.

Matching employment opportunities and expectations . . .
See item no. 360.

Literature

General

468 **The Pāli literature of Ceylon.**
Charles Edmund Godakumbura. Colombo: M. D. Gunasena,
1958. 329p. bibliog.
Studies writings in Pāli, the language of Buddhism, from the 1st century BC to the
1950s.

469 **Sinhalese literature.**
Charles Edmund Godakumbura.   London: University Microfilms
International, 1976. 376p.
A scholarly survey of Sinhalese literature up to the mid-19th century. This work
was first published in 1955 in Sri Lanka.

470 **English literature in Ceylon, 1815-1878.**
Yasmine Gooneratne.   Dehiwala, Sri Lanka: Tisara Prakasakayo,
1968. 234p. bibliog. (*Ceylon Historical Journal*, no. 14).
A critical evaluation of the formative stages of Anglo-Sri Lankan literature, with
particular attention paid to the impact of English ideas and values and to the
dominant forms of literary activity in the period. This is the revised version of the
author's PhD dissertation submitted to Cambridge University.

471 **The Sinhala reading public.**
Marga Institute.   Colombo: Marga Institute, 1974. 70p. (Marga
Research Studies – 4).
Presents the results of a survey carried out by the Marga Institute in relation to its
programme of translating into Sinhalese the major works in modern languages.

The reading habits and reading preferences of the Sinhalese and the trade practices of the publishers as well as the need felt by the Sinhalese intelligentsia for improving their access to modern thought and knowledge are documented.

472 **Martin Wickramasinghe. The sage of Koggala. Essays on the life and work of Martin Wickramasinghe, published on his eighty fifth birthday.**
Dehiwala, Sri Lanka: Tisara Prakasakayo, 1975. 311p.

A felicitation volume presented to the seminal figure in modern Sinhalese literature. Includes ten essays in English paying tribute and evaluating his work as a novelist, critic and essayist. A bibliography of his writings is appended.

473 **Sinhalese verse (kavi) collected by the late Hugh Nevill.**
Hugh Nevill, edited by P. E. P. Deraniyagala. Colombo: Ceylon National Museums Department, 1954-55. 3 vols. (Ceylon National Museums Manuscripts Series, vols. 4, 5, 6).

A catalogue of the Nevill collection of palm-leaf manuscripts in the British Museum which, with over 900 *kavi* of different styles and from different periods, is acknowledged to be the most valuable collection ever assembled. The catalogue provides a description, a representative verse and its English translation.

474 **Sinhalese writing and the new critics.**
Ranjini Obeyesekere. Colombo: M. D. Gunasena, 1974. 119p. bibliog.

This study, which is the revised version of a doctoral dissertation submitted to the University of Washington, Seattle, focuses on the tradition of literary criticism among the Sinhalese and critically examines the work of the major figures in modern literary criticism.

475 **Šigiri graffiti, being Sinhalese verses of the eighth, ninth and tenth centuries.**
Senarat Paranavitana. London: Oxford University Press for the Government of Ceylon, 1956. 2 vols.

A fine translation and scholarly study of the graffiti at Sigiriya, the rock fortress which was turned into a magnificent palace by the Sinhalese king Kassapa who reigned between 473 and 491 AD.

476 **The Sinhalese novel.**
Ediriweera Ranjita Sarathchandra. Colombo: M. D. Gunasena, 1950. 244p.

A critical review of the novel as a literary form by a writer who himself is a distinguished novelist.

477 **Tamil writers in Sri Lanka.**
K. S. Sivakumaran. Colombo: Vijeyaluckshmi Book Depot,
1974. 64p.
The best introduction in the English language to contemporary Tamil writing.

478 **Landmarks of Sinhalese literature.**
Martin Wickramasinghe, translated by Ediriweera Ranjita
Sarathchandra. Colombo: M. D. Gunasena, 1962. 2nd rev. ed.
211p.
Authored by a noted essayist who is also the best known Sinhalese novelist of
contemporary Sri Lanka, this work surveys the development of Sinhalese
literature.

Sri Lanka: a survey.
See item no. 4.

Modern Sri Lanka: a society in transition.
See item no. 5.

History of Ceylon from the beginning of the nineteenth century to 1948.
See item no. 129.

A bibliography of Sri Lankan literature in English.
See item no. 618.

Major writers and translations

479 **Apocalypse 83.**
Jean Arasanayagam. Kandy, Sri Lanka: the author, 1985. 86p.
This collection of poems, devoted to the personal experience of the poet during
the communal troubles of July 1983, powerfully and movingly reveals the anguish
of the innocent victims of ethnic conflict in contemporary Sri Lanka.

480 **Boomerang.**
Mark Bartholomeusz. New York: Carlton Press, 1983. 143p.
For his first published novel, this well-known short-story writer has chosen two
themes which rarely appear in the English-language fiction of Sri Lanka, the
occult and the practice of exorcism among the Sinhalese.

481 **The fountains of paradise.**
   Arthur C. Clarke.   New York, London: Harcourt Brace
   Jovanovich, 1979. 261p.
The Nebula Award winner for 1980, this science fiction is partly set in Sri Lanka, the adopted land of the distinguished writer. Clarke uses Sri Lanka's history and legends to recreate a past which is interwoven with the distant future.

482 **The perfect generosity of Prince Vessantara. A Buddhist epic.**
   Translated from the Pali and illustrated by unpublished paintings
   from Sinhalese temples.
   Margaret Cone, Richard F. Gombrich.   Oxford: Clarendon Press,
   1977. 111p.
A noteworthy translation of the popular *Jataka* (the Buddha's birth) story, which has an important place in the socialization of Buddhist values among the Sinhalese. The illustrations (forty-four plates) are drawn primarily from Buddhist temple murals.

483 **The winds of Sinhala.**
   Colin de Silva.   New York: Doubleday; London: Granada, 1982.
   514p.
A highly romanticized re-telling of the story of King Dutugamunu, the major heroic figure of the Sinhalese whose claim to greatness is based on his defeat of a Tamil usurper of the throne of the Anuradhapura kingdom in the 2nd century BC.

484 **Three women.**
   Chitra Fernando.   Colombo: Lake House Investments, 1983. 55p.
Three short stories with the exploitation of women as their theme.

485 **Selected poems.**
   Patrick Fernando.   Delhi: Oxford University Press, 1985. 64p.
The exclusion of some the poet's best work diminishes the value of this collection.

486 **The call of the kirala.**
   James Goonewardena.   Colombo: Hansa, 1971. 141p.
The flight of the protagonist from the city life to the village is the theme of this well-known novel.

487 **The poetry of Sri Lanka.**
   Edited by Yasmine Gooneratne.   *Journal of South Asian*
   Literature, vol. 12, nos. 1-2 (1976), p. 1-127.
The major poets writing in English and a few writing in Tamil and Sinhalese are represented in this collection. Also included are interviews with poets George Keyt, Patrick Fernando, and Anne Ranasinghe, and an essay on the role of the critic as a translator in Sri Lanka.

488   **Poems from India, Sri Lanka, Malaysia and Singapore.**
      Edited by Yasmine Gooneratne.   Hong Kong, Singapore, Kuala
      Lumpur: Heinemann Asia, 1979. 103p.
Representative poets from Sri Lanka are included in this collection.

489   **Stories from Sri Lanka.**
      Edited by Yasmine Gooneratne.   Hong Kong, Singapore, Kuala
      Lumpur: Heinemann Asia, 1979. 183p.
A collection of short fiction by some of the foremost Sri Lankan writers: Jinadasa
Vijayatunga, Chitra Fernando, James Goonewardena, Anne Ranasinghe,
Punyakante Wijenaike, Tilak Gunawardena and Suvimalee Gunaratna, who
write in English, and Martin Wickramasinghe, A. V. Suraweera, Asoka
Colombage and Gunadasa Amarasekara, who are represented here in English
translation of their writings in Sinhalese. The collection has no representation of
those who write in Tamil.

490   **Bili puja.**
      Suvimalee Gunaratna.   Colombo: Hansa, 1973. 102p.
A collection of short stories by the much acclaimed young writer.

491   **Three characters.**
      K. Jayatillake, translated by Edwin Ariyadasa.   Colombo:
      Pradeepa, 1973. 124p.
Originally published in 1963, this novel by a leading figure in the contemporary
Sinhalese literary scene examines social interaction in a Sinhalese village in the
early part of the 20th century.

492   **Poetry from the Sinhalese; being selections from folk and classical
      poetry, with Sinhalese text.**
      Translated by George Keyt.   Colombo: Colombo Apothecaries,
      1939. 137p.
An anthology worthy of attention, not only for its selections but also for their
sensitive translations.

493   **Forest life in Ceylon.**
      William Knighton.   London: Hurst & Blackett, 1854. 2 vols.
This technically innovative work – it is part memoir, part fiction – which makes a
searching inquiry into the contemporary colonial society is considered a landmark
in the evolution of English literature in Sri Lanka.

494 **An anthology of modern writing from Sri Lanka.**
Edited by Ranjini Obeyesekere, Chitra Fernando. Tucson,
Arizona: University of Arizona Press, 1981. 307p. (Association for
Asian Studies Monograph, no. 38).

A guide to the major Sinhalese writers, and a few writers in English. The
anthology is divided into two sections, covering poetry and prose, with an
introduction to each by the editors. The selections, based on the creativity and
craftsmanship of the writers, are grouped into the writers of the 1950s and of the
1970s.

495 **Running in the family.**
Michael Ondaatje. London: Pan Books, 1984. 207p. map.

This semi-autobiographical account of a journey back to Sri Lanka by the Sri
Lankan-born Canadian poet is evocative of a society which has largely passed
away with the emigration of the Burghers, the community to which the author
belongs. This indeed is a delight to read, with marvellous descriptions of people
and places.

496 **The illicit immigrant.**
Raja Proctor. Colombo: Lake House Investments, 1977. 160p.

The second novel by a writer who has established a solid reputation for his fiction
written in English, this work portrays the hopes and aspirations of an illicit
immigrant from South India and the indignity and abject poverty he faced among
a hostile population in Sri Lanka.

497 **Waiting for Surabiel.**
Raja Proctor. St. Lucia, Queensland, Australia: University of
Queensland Press, 1981. 238p.

Framed within the context of the political developments from the pre-colonial
times to the April 1971 Insurrection, this novel written in English deals with the
changes in rural life and the life story of the protagonist, Surabiel.

498 **Poems.**
Anne Ranasinghe. Colombo: Lake House Investments, 1971.
54p.

An important collection by one of the foremost poets of contemporary Sri Lanka.

499 **An anthology of Sinhalese literature up to 1815 selected by the
UNESCO National Commission of Ceylon.**
Edited with an introduction by Christopher H. B. Reynolds.
London: Allen & Unwin, 1970. 377p. (UNESCO Collection of
Representative Works).

Presents twenty-two works drawn from the rich literature of the Sinhalese and
includes fragments of verses from the 6th to 9th centuries, prose works of the 12th
to 14th centuries, poems of the 15th and 16th centuries and works of the century

before the conquest of the Kandyan kingdom by the British. The introduction examines the literary history of the period.

500 **Pemato jayati soko.** (Love is the bringer of sorrow.)
Ediriweera Ranjita Sarathchandra, translated by Derrick M. de Silva. Salzburg, Austria: Institut für Englishe Sprache und Literatur, Universität Salzburg, 1976. 55p. (Salzburg Studies in English Literature: Poetic Drama and Poetic Theory).

This lyric drama, by the foremost modern Sinhalese playwright and the seminal figure in the resurgence of Sinhalese theatre in post-independent Sri Lanka, was first produced in 1972. Though by no means the best known work of Sarathchandra, this play exemplifies his creativity and the remarkable experimentation he engaged in as a playwright. The story is derived from a book of homilectic tales written by a Buddhist monk in the 14th century and thus, the play concerns itself with issues central to the Buddhist ethical tradition. The translation is exceptional and the translator's lengthy introduction is worthy of special attention, for it discusses the major developments in Sinhalese theatre since the 19th century together with an assessment of Sarathchandra's contributions and his place in the history of modern Sinhalese drama.

501 **Curfew and a full moon.**
Ediriweera Ranjita Sarathchandra. Hong Kong, Singapore, Kuala Lumpur: Heinemann Asia, 1978. 223p. (Writing in Asia Series).

The English-language version of the original work in Sinhalese, this novel explores the relationship between a professor and his students who increasingly commit themselves to revolutionary politics. It is based on life at the University of Ceylon during the April 1971 Insurrection.

502 **Special issue on Sri Lankan literature.**
Edited by Suwanda Suganasiri, A. V. Suraweera. *Toronto South Asia Review*, vol. 3, no. 2 (Fall 1984).

A representative selection of fiction and critical writings by Sri Lankans. Translations from Sinhalese and Tamil and original writings in English are included. The collection claims to exemplify the vibrant, independent and multicultural Sri Lankan literary scene.

503 **Grass for my feet. Vignettes of village life in Sri Lanka.**
Jinadasa Vijayatunga. London: Howard Baker, 1970. 2nd ed. 121p.

First published in 1935, and perhaps the best known fiction work of a Sri Lankan writing in English, this book offers a series of sketches which evoke the tranquillity and simplicity of village Sri Lanka.

504 **Lay bare the roots.**
Martin Wickramasinghe, translated from the Sinhalese by Lakshmi
de Silva. Colombo: M. D. Gunasena, 1968. 112p.

First published in 1940, this celebrated work by the best known novelist of
modern Sri Lanka is beyond doubt the most popular Sinhalese fictional writing in
contemporary Sri Lanka. The story deals with a boy growing up in village Sri
Lanka during a period of rapid economic and social change.

505 **Madol Doova.**
Martin Wickramasinghe, translated by Ashley Halpē. Dehiwala,
Sri Lanka: Tisara Prakasakayo, 1976. 135p.

This popular novel, evoking a bygone era in rural Sri Lanka, was first published
in Sinhalese in 1947.

506 **The waiting earth.**
Punyakante Wijenaike. Colombo: Colombo Apothecaries, 1966.
326p.

The first novel of one of the best known writers in English in Sri Lanka whose
characteristic restrained style and carefully observed detail is very evident here.

507 **The rebel.**
Punyakante Wijenaike. Colombo: Lake House Investments,
1979. 155p.

A collection of short stories. The main story, 'The rebel', has as its setting the
April 1971 Insurrection, a fertile source for fiction in recent times.

508 **Nossa senhora dos Chingalos.** (Our Sinhalese Lady.)
Lakdhasa Wikkramasinha. Colombo: Praja Publishers, 1973.
22p.

This collection brings together the best published poems and several previously
unpublished poems of the young poet who made a tremendous impact on the Sri
Lankan literary scene before his tragic death.

509 **Growing: an autobiography of the years 1904 to 1911.**
Leonard Woolf. New York, London: Harcourt Brace
Jovanovich, 1975. 256p. (Harvest Book – HB 320).

This second volume of Woolf's autobiography covers his stay in Sri Lanka as a
civil servant until he resigned from the service to marry Virginia Stephen. The
experience gained during this period was drawn upon by Woolf for his famous
novel, *The village in the jungle* (q.v.). The volume is revealing of the role of the
British provincial administrators and Woolf's growing disenchantment with British
imperialism.

510   **The village in the jungle. A novel of Ceylon.**
Leonard Woolf, introduction by Evelyn Fredrick Charles
Ludowyk.   Oxford, New York, Toronto, Delhi: Oxford
University Press, 1981. new ed. 179p.

First published in England in 1913 and recognized as a classic of its genre, this
novel drew heavily upon the author's experience as a civil servant in Sri Lanka
(1904-11). A poignant story of the people who inhabit a village in the jungle, it
details their struggles against fate, nature and the forces released by the changes
introduced by British rule, and it symbolizes, according to Woolf himself, the
anti-imperialism which he increasingly began to embrace in his last years as a
colonial administrator. The introduction examines the literary merits of the novel.

The Arts

Visual and perfoming arts

511 **Cultural policy in Sri Lanka.**
H. H. Bandara. Paris: UNESCO, 1972. 70p. (Studies and
Documents on Cultural Policy Series).
Surveys the development of the state machinery for the promotion of cultural
activities, its relationship to the non-state channels of cultural dissemination, and
the cultural activities of the Sinhalese. The author offers no explanation as to why
he does not discuss the cultural activities of the minority communities.

512 **Sinhalese monastic architecture: the viharas of Anurādhapura.**
Senake Bandaranayake. Leiden, The Netherlands: Brill, 1974.
404p. map. bibliog. (Studies in South Asian Culture, Institute of
South Asian Archeology, University of Amsterdam vol. 15).
An important work on the architecture of the Buddhist monasteries of
Anuradhapura, the centre of Sinhalese civilization from the 3rd century BC to the
10th century AD, this study reexamines and interprets the material uncovered by
over 100 years of archaeological research and exploration in Sri Lanka.
Conceptualizing architecture as the substantial and organic expression of a
society, the author delineates the distinctive elements of Sinhalese monastic
architecture, yet also places it within the wider context of the developments which
took place in South and Southeast Asia. The study is in three parts – monastic
plan, building types and architectural form – and 55 plates and 163 figures
illuminate the text. This is a revised version of the author's Oxford University
doctoral thesis.

513 **Furniture of the Dutch period in Ceylon.**
Richard Leslie Brohier. Colombo: National Museums of Ceylon, 1978. 2nd ed. 92p.

The definitive work on the subject. The twenty-seven plates include items from the incomparable collection of Dutch furniture at the National Museum at Colombo.

514 **Mediaeval Sinhalese art: being a monograph on mediaeval Sinhalese arts and crafts mainly as surviving in the eighteenth century with an account of the structure of society, and the status of the craftsmen.**
Ananda Kentish Coomaraswamy. New York: Pantheon, 1956. 2nd ed. 344p.

First published in 1908, this study by the scholar who made seminal contributions to the understanding and appreciation of the arts of Sri Lanka (and of India and Southeast Asia as well) remains the most detailed treatment of the arts of the Sinhalese in the immediate pre-colonial period. It examines not only the achievements of the Sinhalese artists and craftsmen but also attempts to document their training and development and their place in the wider society.

515 **The arts and crafts of India and Ceylon.**
Ananda Kentish Coomaraswamy. New York: Noonday, 1964. new ed. 259p.

A valuable survey of the major and minor arts of Sri Lanka. The discussion is coloured by the author's perspective that culturally Sri Lanka is an integral part of India.

516 **The lonely artist.**
Phillip Coorey. Colombo: Lake House Investments, 1970. 118p.

An evaluation of the work of Lester James Peries, the internationally recognized Sri Lankan film director.

517 **Classical Sinhalese sculpture, 300 B.C. to A.D. 1000.**
Don Titus Devendra. London: Alec Tiranti, 1958. 48p. map.

A survey of development in Sinhalese sculpture in early Sri Lanka, with particular emphasis on the influence of Buddhism.

518 **Ceylon's 43 Group of Painters.**
Ellen Dissanayake. *Arts of Asia*, vol. 16, no. 2 (March-April 1986), p. 61-67.

A survey of the work of the influential groups of painters who deliberately sought to integrate foreign styles with Sri Lankan artistic tradition, thereby creating an art that would be both truly Sri Lankan and truly modern. Representative work from the period between 1943 and 1964, during which the group was active, illustrates the essay.

519   **The Mahayana Buddhist sculpture of Ceylon.**
Diran Kavork Dohanian.   New York, London: Garland, 1977.
167p. bibliog. (Outstanding Dissertations in the Fine Arts – a
Garland Series).

Covering the period from the 7th to the 10th centuries, the author examines, in
this published version of a Harvard University doctoral dissertation, the sculpture
of the Sinhalese, whose distinctive style is to be attributed to the influence of
Mahayana Buddhism.

520   **Masks and mask system of Sri Lanka.**
M. H. Goonatilleka.   Colombo: Tamarind Books, 1978. 96p.

A useful introductory description and discussion of masks used in exorcism and
other rituals in Southwest Sri Lanka.

521   **An album of Buddhist paintings from Sri Lanka (Ceylon) (Kandy
period).**
Siri Gunasinghe.   Colombo: National Museums of Sri Lanka,
1978. 213p.

An introduction to the Buddhist temple murals of the Kandyan period (1469-
1815), with forty plates and explanatory text.

522   **George Keyt: a felicitation volume.**
Edited by Ashley Halpē.   Colombo: George Keyt Felicitation
Committee, 1977. 127p. bibliog.

Issued to mark the seventy-fifth birthday of Sri Lanka's foremost painter, this
volume is devoted to a collective critical assessment of his work. Includes
biographical information and poems and essays by Keyt as well as forty-one
coloured plates and numerous illustrations.

523   **Tamil drama in Ceylon: a tradition usurped.**
Tiru Kandiah.   *South Asian Review*, vol. 5, no. 1 (1971), p. 29-39.

The author contrasts the degeneration of contemporary Tamil drama with the
vitality of contemporary Sinhalese drama, and finds the explanation for this
difference in the specific interests of the Tamil élite which, on the defensive
against both the external threat of Sinhalese nationalism and the internal threat of
social changes, has appropriated tradition as a line of defence with which to
preserve its remaining privileges.

524   **The wooden architecture of Sri Lanka.**
L. K. Karunaratne.   *Ceylon Historical Journal*, vol. 25, nos. 1-4
(1978), p. 174-185.

The distinctive wooden architecture of the Kandyan kingdom, of which several
outstanding examples still remain intact, is examined in this essay.

525 **Mahayanist monuments in Ceylon.**
Nandasena Mudiyanse. Colombo: M. D. Gunasena, 1967. 135p.
The influence of the Mahayana tradition of Buddhism in the art and architecture of the classical civilizations is examined. This is the revised version of the author's University of Ceylon PhD thesis.

526 **The stupa in Ceylon.**
Senarat Paranavitana. Colombo: Government Press, 1946. 105p.
(Memoirs of the Archaeological Survey of Ceylon, vol. 5).
This study, by the scholar whose contribution to the illumination of the early history of Sri Lanka remains unequalled, examines the evolution of the *stupa* (an edifice built over a relic) during the classical period. The emphasis is on the emergence of a distinctive Sinhalese architectural form. Illustrated with twenty-two plates.

527 **Ceylon, paintings from temple, shrine and rock.**
Introduction by Senerat Paranavitana, preface by W. G. Archer.
New York: New York Graphic Society by arrangement with UNESCO, 1957. 52p. (UNESCO World Art Series, vol. 8).
The introduction to this volume on Sinhalese paintings from the 7th to the 19th centuries discusses the technical aspects of the paintings and places them in their historical and cultural context, emphasizing the powerful influence exerted by Buddhism on the Sinhalese artist. Apart from text illustrations, the reader is offered thirty-two magnificent coloured plates, several of which represent the 5th-century frescoes at Sigiriya, generally acknowledged to be the greatest achievements of the Sinhalese artist.

528 **Art of the ancient Sinhalese.**
Senarat Paranavitana. Colombo: Lake House Investments, 1971. 141p.
An excellent introduction to the subject by the eminent scholar of ancient Sri Lanka. The text is supplemented by numerous illustrations.

529 **Some aspects of traditional Sinhalese culture. A symposium.**
Edited by Ralph Pieris. Peradeniya, Sri Lanka: Ceylon University Conference on Traditional Culture, 113p. bibliog.
This collection includes papers on Kandyan dancing and painting, Sinhalese music, puppetry, minor arts and crafts, and on socio-economic and psychological factors which influence cultural dynamism and revival.

530 **Senarat Paranavitana commemoration volume.**
Edited by Leelananda Prematilleke, Karthigesu Indrapala, J. E.
Van Lohuizen-Da Leeuw. Leiden, the Netherlands: Brill, 1978,
300p. bibliog. (Studies in South Asian Culture, vol. 7, Institute of
South Asian Archeology, University of Amsterdam).

Includes several essays on the art and architecture of the classical civilizations,
subjects to which seminal contributions were made by the distinguished scholar
whose work is commemorated. Essays on Sri Lanka's archaeology, history and
language are also to be found, as is a bibliography of Paranavitana's writings
which is revealing of the astonishing depth and breadth of his scholarship.

531 **George Keyt.**
Introduction and biographical note by Martin Russell. Bombay,
India: Marga Publications, 1950. 56p.

An extended discussion of the work of modern Sri Lanka's best known artist,
covering the period from 1927 to 1947. Keyt is viewed as embodying the synthesis
of Indian and European traditions which took place in South Asian art in the 20th
century. Includes 101 plates.

532 **Vihares and verandas Ceylon.**
Barbara Sansoni. Colombo: Barbara Sansoni Fabrics, 1978. 60p.

Covers much more ground than the title indicates: not only the Buddhist temples
and the distinctive features of the Dutch colonial architecture, verandas, are
studied, but also the architectural features of many other public and domestic
structures, from the time of the Kandyan kingdom. Fifty-eight plates of drawings
in black and white are included in this beautifully produced book.

533 **The folk drama of Ceylon.**
Ediriweera Ranjita Sarathchandra. Colombo: Lake House
Investments, 1960. 2nd ed. 180p.

This study describes and places the folk drama of the Sinhalese in its historical
and cultural context, emphasizing the influence of Buddhism and folk beliefs in
the supernatural.

534 **Lionel Wendt's Ceylon.**
Lionel Wendt, introduction by L. C. Van Geyzel, technical note by
Bernard G. Thornley. London: Lincolns-Prager, 1950. 255p.

A portfolio (120 pages) of the work of Sri Lanka's foremost photographer.

Sri Lanka: a survey.
See item no. 4.

Modern Sri Lanka: a society in transition.
See item no. 5.

The perfect generosity of Prince Vessantara . . .
See item no. 482.

Folklore

535 **Folk stories of Sri Lanka.**
George Keyt.   Colombo: Lake House Investments, 1982. 3rd ed.
75p.
A collection of sixteen Sinhalese folk-tales translated into English and illustrated
with lively line drawings by the foremost Sri Lankan painter.

536 **Village folk-tales of Ceylon.**
Collected and translated by Henry Parker.   London: Luzac,
1910-1914. 3 vols.
The most extensive collection of Sinhalese folk-tales, fables and legends available
in print.

537 **Folk tales of Sri Lanka.**
Manel Ranatunga.   New Delhi: Sterling Publishers, 1980. 2nd ed.
118p. (Folk Tales of the World, no. 9).
A re-telling in English of thirty-three popular folk-tales drawn from the Sinhalese,
Tamil and Muslim communities.

Rituals and festivals

538 **The festivals of Ceylon.**
C. M. Austin de Silva. *Spolia Zeylanica*, vol. 31, no. 2 (1969),
p. 359-80.
Describes the major social and religious festivals in Sri Lanka.

539 **Sinhalese festivals, their symbolism, origins and proceedings.**
Charles Edmund Godakumbura.   *Journal of the Ceylon Branch of
the Royal Asiatic Society*, new series, vol. 14 (1970), p. 91-130.
An examination and analysis of the main Buddhist annual festivals and rituals.

540 **Sri Lanka. The Kandy perahara.**
Victor Ratnavale. Hong Kong: West-Pacific Associates Private, 1978. 112p.

Presents reproductions of colour photographs of the *perahara*, the most important ritual of the Temple of the Tooth in Kandy. The photographs amply convey the magnificence of this annual pageant which is perhaps the largest and most elaborate ritual in the Buddhist world.

541 **Kataragama. The holiest place in Ceylon.**
Paul Wirz. translated by Doris Berta Pralle. Colombo: Lake House Investments, 1972. 2nd ed. 57p. bibliog.

Studies the structure of the places of worship, traditions and legends, and rituals and festivals associated with the god Kataragama, worshipped by Buddhists and Hindus as well as by some Muslims are described in this work. The original appeared in German in 1954.

The Kataragama pilgrimage: Hindu-Buddhist interaction and its significance in Sri Lanka's polyethnic social system.
See item no. 207.

Rituals of the Kandyan state.
See item no. 213.

Sports

542 **The rifle and hound in Ceylon.**
Samuel White Baker. New York: Arno Press, 1967. 409p.
(Abercrombie & Fitch Library).
This work on the sporting activities of the British colonial community, by the famed explorer who participated in them, was first published in 1854 in London by Longman, Brown, Green and Longmans.

543 **Hunting and shooting in Ceylon.**
Harry Storey. Dehiwala, Sri Lanka: Tisara Prakasakayo, 1969. 275p.
The classic work on the popular sports of the 19th-century colonial society. The reprint does not include about half of the illustrations of the original, and thus the reader may wish to consult the first edition (365p. + 35 plates) published in 1907 by Longmans, Green in London and New York.

Eight years in Ceylon.
See item no. 35.

Needs of children and adolescents. A case study of Sri Lanka.
See item no. 263.

Libraries, Museums and Archives

544   Libraries and people. Colombo Public Library 1925-1975. A commemorative volume.
Colombo Public Library.   Colombo: Colombo Public Library, 1975. 282p.
The development of libraries in Sri Lanka is examined in this collection of essays. Both public and university libraries are considered, and the Colombo Public Library, the premier public library in the country, receives special attention.

545   Colombo Museum 1877-1977. Hundred years souvenir.
Compiled by P. H. D. H. de Silva.   Colombo: Department of National Museums, 1977. 148p.
The history of the Colombo Museum and the role it has played in educational and cultural life since its establishment are the themes covered in this collection of essays.

546   The Sri Lankan collection.
Vidya Dehejia.   *Arts of Asia*, vol. 15, no. 6 (Dec. 1985), p. 80-89.
This article describes (with illustrations) the Sri Lankan art collection at the Los Angeles County Museum of Art, a collection which is perhaps surpassed only by those at the British Museum and the Museum of Fine Arts in Boston.

547   Directory of scientific and technical libraries in Sri Lanka.
National Science Council of Sri Lanka.   Colombo: Sri Lanka Scientific and Technical Information Centre, National Science Council of Sri Lanka, 1977. 63p.
A useful guide to the specialized libraries.

146

548 **Register of museums and collections of antiquities in Sri Lanka.**
Sri Lanka. Ministry of Cultural Affairs. Colombo: Department of
Government Printing, 1974. 107p.
A valuable guide to museums and institutions which have holdings of antiquities.
Its inclusion of Buddhist temples, which though not professionally organized have
in their possession important antiquities, is especially noteworthy.

549 **Cambridge South Asian archives. Records of the British period in
South Asia relating to India, Pakistan, Ceylon, Burma, Nepal and
Afghanistan held at the Centre of South Asian Studies, University of
Cambridge.**
Compiled and edited by Mary Thatcher. London: Mansell, 1973.
346p.
Material on Sri Lanka, mainly the papers of ex-Ceylon civil servants, is described
and indexed in this guide.

550 **A guide to Western manuscripts and documents in the British Isles
relating to South and South-east Asia.**
Compiled by M. D. Wainwright, Noel Matthews. London:
Oxford University Press for the School of Oriental and African
Studies, University of London, 1965, 523p.
The invaluable guide to material on Sri Lanka in British collections, including the
principal collection, the Colonial Office records at the Public Records Office.

551 **An introduction to the national archives – Sri Lanka.**
K. D. G. Wimalaratne. Colombo: National Science Council of
Sri Lanka, 1978. 32p. bibliog.
A survey of the development, functions and organization of Sri Lanka's national
archives. Appendixes list its holdings and the arrangement of its Dutch archives.

**Education in Ceylon (from the sixth century B.C. to the present day). A
centenary volume.**
See item no. 451.

**Sri Lanka (Ceylon) since independence (1948-1976): a bibliographical
survey of the literature in Sri Lanka in the field of the social sciences.**
See item no. 623.

Mass Media

General

552 Communication policies in Sri Lanka.
M. A. de Silva, Reggie Siriwardene. Paris: UNESCO, 1977. 59p.
(Communication Policies Studies).

This report, by a committee appointed by the Ministry of Education, provides general information and relevant statistical data relating to the communication policies of the government of Sri Lanka.

553 The taming of the press in Sri Lanka.
Shelton Abeywickreme Gunaratne. *Journalism Monographs*, no. 39 (May 1975), p. 1-42.

A somewhat perfunctory examination of the efforts of successive Sri Lanka Freedom Party governments to control the press, which culminated with the take-over of the Lake House Group, the largest and most powerful newspaper publisher in Sri Lanka, in 1973. The introductory section of the essay offers a useful discussion of the characteristics of the Sri Lanka press as it stood in 1973.

554 Sri Lanka.
Shelton Abeywickreme Gunaratne. In: *Newspapers in Asia*. Edited by John A. Lent. Hong Kong, Singapore, Kuala Lumpur: Heinemann Asia, 1982, p. 506-36. (Asian Studies Series).

The characteristics of the press in Sri Lanka and the government-press conflict, which arose in the mid-1960s and culminated with the government taking control of the newspapers of the powerful Lake House Group in 1973, are examined in this essay.

148

555   **Ceylon.**
      Herbert Alexander Jayatilleke Hulugalle. In: *The Asian*
      newspapers' reluctant revolution. Edited by John A. Lent.   Ames,
      Iowa: Iowa University Press, 1971, p. 259-67.
This short essay, by a distinguished journalist, traces the history of newspapers in
Sri Lanka.

556   **The Ceylonese press and the fall of the Sirimavo Bandaranaike**
      government.
      Raymond E. Vickery, Jr.   *South Atlantic Quarterly*, vol. 66, no. 3
      (Summer 1967), p. 424-39.
The thrust of the argument presented in this essay is that the attempts of the
Bandaranaike government to control the press, in particular the dominant Lake
House group of newspapers, was the decisive and immediate factor in its fall in
December 1964. This single-factor explanation is highly questionable, though the
importance of the adverse impact the attempt to control the press had on the
parliamentary fortunes of the Bandaranaike government should not be over-
looked.

557   **Press and politics in Sri Lanka.**
      W. A. Wiswa Warnapala.   *Journal of Constitutional and*
      Parliamentary Studies, vol. 9, no. 2 (April-June 1975), p. 125-55.
      1975), p. 125-55.
The role played by the powerful family-owned newspapers in Sri Lanka's political
process and the factors which gave rise to attempts to impose state control on
them are discussed. The first major legislation on the press, the Press Council Act
of 1973, is also discussed.

Newspapers

558   **Daily News.**
      Colombo, 1918-. daily (except Sunday).
This newspaper, which was originally known as the *Ceylon Daily News*, was the
most influential English-language daily until its publisher, the powerful Lake
House Group, was taken over by the government in 1973. Since then its editorial
policy has reflected government opinion. It now has a daily circulation of 65,000.

559   **The Island.**
      1981-. daily (except Sunday).
Within a short span of five years, this newspaper has achieved a remarkable
success – its daily circulation now stands at 115,000 – and it has eclipsed the older,
established English-language dailies. Much of its success is owed to its
investigative journalism and to its critical approach towards the government.

560 **Observer.**
    Colombo, 1834-. daily.

One of the oldest English-language newspapers of Asia, this has been a government-owned publication since 1973.

561 **Sun.**
    Colombo, 1964-. daily.

This newspaper was closed down by the government between 1974 and 1977 and it has not been successful in regaining the ground lost during those years. It currently has the smallest circulation of the English-language newspapers in Sri Lanka.

562 **Sunday Island.**
    1981-. Sunday.

The Sunday version of *The Island* (*see* entry no. 559). With a circulation of 325,000, it has the widest circulation of the newspapers in Sri Lanka.

563 **Weekend.**
    Colombo, 1965-. Sunday.

Issued in tabloid form, this newspaper is primarily devoted to the arts and entertainment.

Periodicals
and
Directories

564 Ancient Ceylon, Journal of the Archeological Survey Department of Sri Lanka.
Colombo: Department of Archeological Survey, 1971-. annual.
A journal devoted to research on prehistoric Sri Lanka.

565 Annual Report of the Monetary Board to the Minister of Finance.
Colombo: Central Bank of Sri Lanka. 1949-. annual.
This statutorily required report annually reviews the economy of Sri Lanka.

566 Central Bank Bulletin.
Colombo: Central Bank of Sri Lanka, 1949-. monthly.
A monthly review of developments in the economy, supplemented with a statistical appendix.

567 Central Bank Staff Studies.
Colombo: Central Bank of Sri Lanka, 1971-. semi-annual.
The research journal of the Central Bank of Sri Lanka.

568 Ceylon Historical Journal.
Dehiwala, Sri Lanka: Tisara Prakasakayo, 1951-. quarterly.
In recent years this journal has been published annually (incorporating four issues), and includes reprints of 19th-century works of history and travel descriptions as well as new historical monographs.

569 **Ceylon Journal of Historical and Social Studies.**
Peradeniya, Sri Lanka: Ceylon Historical and Social Studies
Publications Board, 1958-, new series, 1971-. irregular.
The premier journal in the social sciences.

570 **Economic Review.**
Colombo: Research Department, People's Bank, 1974-. monthly.
Contemporary economic, social and political issues are addressed in this
publication.

571 **Economic and Social Statistics of Sri Lanka.**
Colombo: Central Bank of Sri Lanka, 1978-. semi-annual.
General socio-economic data as well as results of special surveys undertaken by
the Central Bank on the socio-economic conditions of Sri Lanka are published in
this periodical. A valuable tool for the researcher.

572 **Epigraphia Zeylanica, being lithic and other inscriptions of Ceylon.**
Colombo: Archeological Survey of Ceylon, 1904-. irregular.
This periodical presents to the reader inscriptions – an invaluable source for the
reconstruction of Sri Lanka's past – as they are discovered, transliterated, and
translated by the staff of the Archeological Survey. Thus far, five complete
volumes have been published and the sixth volume's first number was issued in
1973.

573 **Epigraphical Notes.**
Colombo: Department of Archeology, 1972-. monthly.
Information about new discoveries in epigraphy and the text and translation of
inscriptions are given in this publication.

574 **Exponews.**
Colombo: Trade Information Service, Department of Commerce,
1976-. monthly.
A monthly newsletter on Sri Lanka's exports and on export prospects.

575 **Ferguson's Sri Lanka Directory.**
Colombo: Associated Newspapers of Sri Lanka, 1859-. annual.
The oldest continuously published and by far the most useful general reference
work on Sri Lanka, this provides current information about the political and
economic situation in the country, statistics and data on such subjects as trade,
agricultural products, industry and government expenditure, detailed information
on plantations, a 'who's who' and a listing of professionals in Sri Lanka.
Originally titled *Ceylon Summary of Useful Information and Plantation Gazetteer*,
it has undergone many changes in title but its format has remained substantially
the same since the 1860 issue.

576 **Journal of Development Administration.**
Colombo: Sri Lanka Institute for Development Administration,
1970-. bi-annual.
The successor to the *Training Digest*, a quarterly published between 1968-69.
Reports on state efforts, through the Institute, to retrain the bureaucracy for
development-oriented work.

577 **Journal of the Dutch Burgher Union.**
Colombo: Dutch Burgher Union, 1908-. quarterly.
This publication is primarily devoted to the history of Dutch rule and the history
and genealogy of the Dutch Burgher community.

578 **Journal of the National Agricultural Society of Sri Lanka.**
Peradeniya, Sri Lanka: National Agricultural Society of Sri Lanka,
1963-. annual.
Before the title change in 1972 this was the *Journal of the National Agricultural
Society of Ceylon.*

579 **Journal of the National Education Society of Sri Lanka.**
Peradeniya, Sri Lanka: National Education Society of Sri Lanka,
1951-. annual.
Until the 1974 issue this publication appeared as the *Journal of the National
Education Society of Ceylon.*

580 **Journal of the National Science Council of Sri Lanka.**
Colombo: National Science Council of Sri Lanka, 1973-. bi-annual.
The research journal of this Council which is the government-sponsored
organization mandated to promote science in Sri Lanka.

581 **Journal of the Sri Lanka Branch of the Royal Asiatic Society.**
Colombo: Royal Asiatic Society (Sri Lanka Branch), 1847-. new
series, 1950-. annual.
This is the oldest continuously published scholarly journal in Sri Lanka. Until
1974 its title was the *Journal of the Ceylon Branch of the Royal Asiatic Society.*

582 **Karmāntha.**
Colombo: Industrial Development Board of Sri Lanka, 1974-.
monthly.
A publication devoted to industry and industrial development in Sri Lanka.

583 **Lanka Guardian.**
Colombo: Lanka Guardian Publishing Company, 1978-.
fortnightly.
A journal of current news and commentary.

584 **Logos.**
Colombo: Centre for Society and Religion. 1962-. quarterly.
This publication by the Roman Catholic Church-oriented activist study centre is devoted to addressing contemporary social, economic and political issues.

585 **Loris: A Journal of Sri Lanka Wild Life.**
Colombo: Wildlife and Nature Protection Society of Sri Lanka, 1936-. semi-annual.
Several important studies of Sri Lanka's wildlife have appeared in this journal over the years. It has also performed a valuable educative service in drawing attention to the wider public issues affecting wildlife, and in particular those developments which have had an adverse effect on the country's wildlife sanctuaries.

586 **Marga.**
Colombo: Marga Institute, 1971-. quarterly.
The journal of the well-known centre for development studies in Sri Lanka.

587 **Modern Ceylon Studies.**
Peradeniya, Sri Lanka: University of Peradeniya, 1970-. irregular.
The successor, in the field of social science research, to the *University of Ceylon Review* 1943-67.

588 **Directory of scientific research projects in Sri Lanka, 1970-1973.**
National Science Council of Sri Lanka. Colombo: National Science Council of Sri Lanka, 1974. 400p.
A valuable but incomplete listing of scientific research completed or being carried out at the universities and government research institutions.

589 **Navasilu. Journal of the English Association of Sri Lanka and the Association for Commonwealth Literature and Language Studies, Sri Lanka.**
Peradeniya, Sri Lanka: English Association of Sri Lanka, 1977-. annual.
The major journal devoted to English literature in Sri Lanka.

590 **New Ceylon Writing.**
Sydney: the editor (Yasmine Gooneratne), 1971-. annual.
A publication devoted to new creative writing in English in prose and verse and criticism.

154

591 **New Law Reports.**
Colombo: Government Printer, 1896-. bi-monthly.
This periodical carries the reports of more important cases decided by the higher appellate courts in Sri Lanka.

592 **Proceedings of the Sri Lanka Association for the Advancement of Science.**
Colombo: Sri Lanka Association for the Advancement of Science, 1944-. annual.
The research papers presented at the annual meeting of the premier scientific association are presented in this publication. Previously entitled *Proceedings of the Ceylon Association for the Advancement of Science.*

593 **Public Investment.**
Colombo: National Planning Division, Ministry of Finance and Planning, 1980-. annual.
Covers the subject of public sector investments.

594 **Register of recent and on-going research in economic and social development in Sri Lanka.**
Colombo: Centre for Development Information, Ministry of Finance and Planning, 1982-. annual.
This publication covers current development research carried out both in Sri Lanka and in other countries. The failure to provide full bibliographical information limits its usefulness.

595 **Review of the Economy.**
Colombo: Central Bank of Sri Lanka, 1975-. annual.
The detailed analysis of economic trends and developments made annually by Sri Lanka's Central Bank.

596 **Spolia Zeylanica: Bulletin of the National Museums of Sri Lanka.**
Colombo: Department of National Museums, 1903-. semi-annual.
One of Sri Lanka's leading scholarly publications, this is the research journal of the staff of the National Museums.

597 **Sri Lanka Coconut Quarterly.**
Bandirippuwa, Sri Lanka: Coconut Research Institute of Sri Lanka, 1954-. quarterly.
Until the title change in 1972 was *Ceylon Coconut Quarterly*.

598   **Sri Lanka Government Gazette.**
Colombo: Government Printer, 1802-. weekly.
This government publication carries official notices, proclamations and regulations. Until 1972 its title was *Ceylon Government Gazette.*

599   **Sri Lanka Journal of Agricultural Studies.**
Colombo: Agrarian Research and Training Institute, 1980-.
The journal of the foremost research centre in the agrarian sector of Sri Lanka.

600   **Sri Lanka Journal of the Humanities.**
Peradeniya, Sri Lanka: University of Peradeniya, 1970-. semi-annual.
The successor, in the field of humanities, to the *University of Ceylon Review*, 1943-67.

601   **Sri Lanka Journal of the Social Sciences.**
Colombo: National Science Council of Sri Lanka, 1978-. semi-annual.
The publication of the Social Science Research Centre established by the National Science Council to promote research in the social sciences in Sri Lanka.

602   **Sri Lanka Journal of South Asian Studies.**
Jaffna, Sri Lanka: University of Jaffna, 1979-. annual.
Although this social science journal was established with a specific regional focus, it has carried, in the main, articles relating exclusively to Sri Lanka.

603   **Sri Lanka Labour Gazette.**
Colombo: Department of Labour, 1949-. monthly.
This official publication, titled *Ceylon Labour Gazette* between 1949 and 1972, carries articles on issues relevant to labour relations, information on laws and administrative regulations affecting labour, and decisions of Labour Tribunals.

604   **Sri Lanka National Bibliography.**
Colombo: Sri Lanka National Library Services Board, 1962-. quarterly.
This was entitled *Ceylon National Bibliography* until 1972.

605   **Sri Lanka News.**
Colombo: Associated Newspapers, 1979-. weekly.
A weekly digest of news from Sri Lanka for the overseas reader.

606   **Sri Lanka Today.**
Colombo: Department of Information, 1972-. monthly.
Previously published as *Ceylon Today*, 1952-1972, this is the government of Sri Lanka's main news publication.

607   **The Sri Lanka Year Book.**
Colombo: Department of Census and Statistics, 1948-. annual.
This is the Sri Lanka government's statistical annual and commentary on the social, economic and general conditions of the country. Until 1972 its title was *The Ceylon Year Book.*

608   **Statistical Abstract of Sri Lanka.**
Colombo: Department of Census and Statistics, 1949-. annual.
Previously titled *Statistical Abstract of Ceylon*, (1949-72), this is the Sri Lanka government's annual statistical compendium.

609   **The Statistical Pocket Book of Sri Lanka.**
Colombo: Department of Census and Statistics, 1966-. annual.
A shorter and condensed version of the *Statistical Abstract of Sri Lanka* (q.v.). From 1966 to 1972 it was titled the *Statistical Pocketbook of Ceylon.*

610   **Tea Quarterly.**
Talawakelle, Sri Lanka: Tea Research Institute of Sri Lanka, 1928-. quarterly.
The research journal of the internationally-known research institute.

611   **Tribune. A journal of Ceylon and World Affairs.**
Colombo: Tribune Publishers, 1954-. weekly.
A Left-oriented weekly which offers news and commentary on Sri Lanka and world affairs.

612   **Tropical Agriculturist.**
Peradeniya, Sri Lanka: Department of Agriculture, 1881-. semi-annual.
One of the most important and influential publications during British times, this journal has had to compete with several other research journals in the field of agriculture in post-independent Sri Lanka.

613   **University of Ceylon Review.**
Peradeniya, Sri Lanka: University of Ceylon, 1943-67. quarterly.
During its more than two decades of existence, this was Sri Lanka's best known research journal in the field of the social sciences. It functioned as the principal publication source for the research carried out by the members of the Social Science Faculty of the University of Ceylon.

614 **University of Colombo Review.**
Colombo: University of Colombo, 1981-. annual.
The research journal of the Faculties of Arts, Science, Education, Law and Medicine of the University of Colombo.

615 **Vidyodaya Journal of Arts, Science and Letters.**
Nugegoda, Sri Lanka: University of Jayewardenepura, 1969-. annual.
The research journal of the University of Jayewardenepura.

Bibliographies and Indexes

616 **Bibliography of scientific publications relating to Sri Lanka 1960-1976.**
A. W. A. T. Alwis. Colombo: Social Science Research Centre, National Science Council of Sri Lanka, 1978. 244p.
A pioneering bibliography with 2,335 entries which illustrates the impressive work which has been carried out in the pure sciences by both Sri Lankan and foreign scholars. No annotations are provided.

617 **A catalogue of postgraduate theses available in the university and research libraries of Sri Lanka.**
Compiled and edited by Niltolange Amarasinghe. Colombo: Ceylon National Library Services Board, 1978. 197p. (Ceylon National Library Services Board Publications, no. 3).
A full listing of dissertations accepted by Sri Lankan and foreign universities for graduate degrees and available for consultation in the institutions named.

618 **A bibliography of Sri Lankan literature in English.**
S. Bertram Bandara. In: *Asia/Pacific Literature in English, Bibliographies*. Edited by Robert E. McDowell, Judith M. McDowell. Washington, DC: Three Continents Press, 1978, p. 1-28.
The only bibliography of its kind.

619 **Land, maps and surveys: descriptive catalogue of historical maps in the Surveyor-General's Office.**
Richard Leslie Brohier, Jan Hendrick Oliver Paulusz. Colombo: Ceylon Government Press, 1951. 2 vols.

A valuable descriptive index to the historical maps in the Surveyor-General's Office as well as in the Colombo Museum and National Archives.

620 **The history of Ceylon (c. 1500-1658): a historiographical and bibliographical survey.**
Chandra Richard de Silva, Daya de Silva. *Ceylon Journal of Historical and Social Studies*, new series, vol. 3, no. 1 (Jan.-June 1973), p. 52-77.

Surveys the historical sources and writings relating to the period of Portuguese rule in Sri Lanka. The bibliography lists 340 entries, some with annotations.

621 **Industrial Ceylon: a select bibliography.**
Daya de Silva. Colombo: Industrial Development Board, 1970. 161p.

With over 1,000 unannotated entries, this bibliography covers a wide range of literature, including books, periodical articles, and government documents. Particularly useful are its citations of mimeographed material available at the Industrial Development Board's library.

622 **A bibliography of manuscripts relating to Ceylon in the archives and libraries of Portugal.**
Daya de Silva. Colombo: H. W. Cave, 1972. 149p.

A valuable tool for the researcher on Portuguese rule in Sri Lanka. This bibliography first appeared in *Boletim Internacional de Bibliografia Luso-Brasileira*, vol. 8, no. 3 (1967), p. 533-52; vol. 8, no. 4 (1967), p. 647-75; vol. 9, no. 1 (1968), p. 84-157; vol. 9, no. 2 (1968), p. 499-527.

623 **Sri Lanka (Ceylon) since independence (1948-1976): a bibliographical survey of the literature in Sri Lanka in the field of the social sciences.**
Compiled by Daya de Silva, Chandra Richard de Silva, edited by the Asia Documentation Center, Hamburg. Hamburg, GFR: Institute of Asian Affairs, 1978. 172p.

Offers 1,611 entries, some with sketchy annotations. The brief introduction draws attention to the major writings in the different fields and to the libraries in Sri Lanka which hold substantial material in the social sciences.

624   A bibliography of Ceylon: a systematic guide to the literature on the land, people, history and culture published in the Western languages from the sixteenth century to the present day.
Henry Alfred Ian Goonetileke.   Zug, Switzerland: Inter-Documentation, 1970-83. 5 vols. (Bibliotheca Asiatica, 5, 14, 16).

The publication of the first two volumes of this on-going project in 1970 was undoubtedly a major event in the scholarship on Sri Lanka, and this bibliography quickly established itself as an indispensable tool for the researcher on Sri Lanka. The volumes which have so far appeared cover the litrature up to 1978 and contain over 26,000 entries. Entries are generally annotated and are of varying quality and length, and it is to be noted that the compiler's goal of comprehensiveness has led to the inclusion of material of questionable value.

625   The April 1971 insurrection in Ceylon, a bibliographical commentary.
Henry Alfred Ian Goonetileke.   Louvain, Belgium: Centre de Recherches Socio-Religieuses, Université de Louvain, 1975. 2nd ed. 98p.

A select bibliography of the writings in the Western languages on the 1971 Insurrection. Contains 440 entries extensively annotated. Also included are 25 photographs which illustrate the insurgency and 25 reproductions of the murals drawn in the detention camp by the insurgents which convey powerful and revealing images of the insurgency and its background.

626   Mass communication in Sri Lanka: an annotated bibliography.
Compiled by Henry Alfred Ian Goonetileke, Samuel Devasirivadhan, Ariyaratne Senadeera.   Singapore: Asian Mass Communication Research and Information Center, 1978. 77p. (Bibliography Series – 9).

The 362 entries in this compilation cover publications in Sinhalese, Tamil and English which appeared in the period 1945 to 1973.

627   July 1983 and the national question in Sri Lanka: a bibliographical guide.
Henry Alfred Ian Goonetileke.   *Race and Class*, vol. 26, no. 1 (summer 1984), p. 159-93.

A comprehensive bibliography – 572 entries – of the writings pertaining to the events of July 1983 which saw unparalleled Sinhalese mob attacks on the minority Tamils. Both academic and popular writings are included but no annotations are provided.

628   **An index to periodical articles on the laws of Ceylon.**
Barry Metzger.   Colombo: H. W. Cave, 1972. 238p.

Covers journals published in Sri Lanka (1845-1971), with separate subject and author indexes.

629   **South Asian civilization. A bibliographic synthesis.**
Maureen L. P. Patterson, in collaboration with William J.
Alspaugh.   Chicago; London: University of Chicago Press, 1981.
853p. 2 maps.

Sri Lanka is treated extensively in this bibliography. There are no annotations, and the entries reflect an uncritical approach, for many publications of little or limited value have been included.

630   **A bibliography on health in Sri Lanka, 1979-1980.**
Kamalika Pieris, C. G. Uragoda.   Colombo: Ceylon College of
Physicians, 1983. 164p.

This bibliography, with 5,500 entries, covers health and disease in Sri Lanka, and includes references to Western as well as traditional healing systems practised in the country.

631   **A bibliography of socio-economic studies in the agrarian sector of
Sri Lanka.**
Compiled by W. Ranasinghe, S. M. K. Mileham, C. Gunatunga.
Colombo: Agrarian Training and Research Institute, 1977. 208p.

This specialist bibliography, with 2,305 entries, is particularly useful because of its inclusion of unpublished papers and reports and publications, such as those of the Agriculture Training and Research Institute, which have limited circulation. However, the reader should be mindful that this compilation fails to meet many accepted bibliographical standards.

Index

The index is a single alphabetical sequence of authors (personal and corporate), titles of publications and subjects. Index entries refer both to the main items and to other works mentioned in the notes to each item. Title entries are in italics. Numeration refers to the items as numbered.

168

History *contd.*
  land tenure 410, 413, 419
  language 178-180, 187, 190, 193
  law 152, 322, 325, 328-347
  library 544
  Marxism 75, 155-156
  mediaeval 78, 85, 88, 90-91, 99-101,
    419, 514
  museums 545
  nationalism 119, 150-151, 158, 165,
    180, 270, 273-274, 277-278, 300,
    449, 523
  periodicals 564, 568-569, 577
  police 130, 147
  politics 79, 81, 89, 100, 127, 150,
    284, 286, 299-305, 308-314
  population 166, 168, 171-175
  Portuguese expulsion 104, 116-117
  Portuguese rule 102, 104, 106, 111,
    114-117, 457, 620, 622
  post-independence 1, 138, 155-165
  pre-colonial 78, 81, 96, 514
  prehistoric 25, 57-60, 96
  pre-1948 2, 119, 129, 134-135, 138,
    150, 154
  press 553-557
  race riots 161, 275, 281-282, 479,
    627
  railways 29, 409
  Rebellion (1818) 146, 148
  religion 79, 102, 104-106, 128, 158,
    204-206, 209, 212, 214-216, 218,
    222-225
  roads 153
  sculpture 517, 519
  Sinhalese kingdoms 94, 100, 137
  social 68, 87, 170, 236
  Stone Age 57
  Tamil 89, 97, 118, 128, 132, 149
  transport and communications 118,
    120, 408-409
  treaties 108, 351-353
History of the birds of Ceylon 48
History of Buddhism in Ceylon 98
History of Ceylon 96
History of the Ceylon civil service,
  1802-1833 136
History of Ceylon from the beginning
  of the nineteenth century to 1948
  129
History of the Ceylon police 130, 147
History of kingship in Ceylon up to the

fourth century A.D. 92
History of the Methodist Church in
  Ceylon, 1814-1964 222
History of the Public Works
  Department, Ceylon 1796-1913
  408
History of the Sinhalese noun 194
History of Sri Lanka 58
Hocart, A. M. 67
Homicide 245, 256
Homilectic tales 500
Horowitz, D. L. 159
Hoselitz, B. F. 371
Housing 246, 264
Housing in Sri Lanka 264
Houtart, F. 204-205, 221
Hulugalle, H. A. J. 30, 134, 555
Humanities journal 600
Hundred years of Ceylon tea,
  1867-1967 432
Hundred years of Ceylonese in
  Malaysia and Singapore
  (1867-1967) 132
Hundred years of local government in
  Ceylon (1865-1965) 318
Hunting and shooting in Ceylon 543

I

Ideology 79, 225
  political 300, 311, 353
Ideology of popular justice in Sri
  Lanka 344
Illicit immigrant 496
Illustrations 3, 14-15, 29-30, 38, 534
  April 1971 insurrection 625
  architecture 512, 526, 532
  art 482, 522, 527-528, 531, 546
  field sports 543
  flora and fauna 36, 45, 48, 52, 54
  folklore 535
  furniture 513
  Kandyan kingdom 40
  pageantry 540
  photographs 29, 36, 38, 534, 540,
    625
Images of Ceylon through American
  eyes 38
Immigrants
  hostility towards 496
  Indian 118, 128, 149, 232, 349, 496

179

Lawrie, A. C. 137
Laws and customs of the Tamils of Jaffna 340
Lay bare the roots 504
Leach, E. R. 229, 240
Leaders, Nationalist 135, 144, 150, 333
Lear, Edward 39
Learmouth, A. M. 19
Learmouth, A. T. A. 19
Lebbe, M. W. Ishak 250
Legal framework of industrial relations in Ceylon 446
Legal system
  pre-independence 129, 152, 328-332, 338, 343, 346, 413
  post-independence 4, 322-327, 333-337, 339-342, 344-345, 347
Legal system of Ceylon in its historical setting 337
Legends 79, 481, 483, 536, 541
Legge, W. V. 48
Legislators 298
Legislators and representation in Sri Lanka 298
Legislatures of Ceylon, 1928-1948 338
Leitan, T. G. R. 319
Lemercinier, G. 221
Lent, J. A. 554-555
Lerski, G. J. 296
Leslie, C. 267
Levesque, J. 311
Lewis, J. P. 70
Liberation of the village 242
Libraries 451, 544, 547, 617
  Colombo Public Library 544
  Industrial Development Board 621
  Portuguese 622
  social sciences holdings 623
Libraries and people. Colombo Public Library 1925-1975 544
Life and customs 1-14
  caste 128, 162, 229, 232, 234-236, 241, 273, 279, 291
  ceremonies 28, 213, 226-228, 533, 538-541
  folklore 228, 533, 535-537
  kinship 113, 168, 234, 229-230, 240-241, 413
  marriage 113, 125, 229-230, 241, 339, 413
Lim, Y. 401

Linguistic nationalism 180, 273-274, 277-278
Linguistic studies 178-182, 184-185, 188-195
Linguistics in South Asia 182
Lionel Wendt's Ceylon 534
List of tombstones and monuments in Ceylon 70
Literature 4, 129, 590
  drama 500
  English-language 470-471, 480, 487, 493-494, 496-497, 502-503, 506, 509-510, 589-590
  essays 472
  fables 536
  folk-tales 535-537
  historical chronicles 78-83, 88, 214, 216, 468
  history in 481, 483
  homilectic tales 500
  kavi 473, 499
  legends in 79, 481, 483, 536
  literary criticism 470, 474, 476, 502, 590
  memoirs 6, 133, 153-154, 493, 495, 509
  novels 480-481, 483-484, 486, 489-491, 493, 496-497, 501, 503-507, 510
  Pāli 78-84, 216, 468
  periodicals 564-615
  poetry 473, 475, 479, 485, 487-488, 492, 498, 508
  poets 479, 485, 487-488, 494-495, 498, 508
  readership 471
  science fiction 481
  short stories 484, 489-490, 507
  Sinhalese 5, 85, 469, 471-475, 478, 487, 491-492, 494, 499-505
  Tamil 66, 477, 487, 502
  translations 471, 473, 482, 500-502, 505, 535, 537, 541
  travellers' accounts 35-43, 568
  writers 472, 476-478, 480-481, 489-490, 494, 496, 500, 504, 509-510
Literary criticism 470, 474, 476, 502, 590
Literary language
  Sinhalese 178, 186
Literary Sinhalese 186

184

Siriweera, W. I. 419
Sivakumaran, K. S. 477
*Sketch of the constitution of the
    Kandyan Kingdom* 329
Skinner, A. 153
Skinner, T. 153
Skjønsberg, E. 239
Slavery
    missionary work against 128
Small, W. J. T. 222
Smith, B. L. 214-216
Smith, D. E. 305
Smith, T. E. 173
Snodgrass, D. R. 369
Social change 5, 68
    and suicide 248
    British colonial period 129
    Muslim 224
    post-independence 242-256, 358
    Tamil 523
Social development
    British rule 126
    post-independence 355
    research 594
Social groups 229-239
    aristocracy 107
    Burghers 231, 233, 495, 577
    children 257, 263
    class identity 297
    coir workers 251
    élites 129, 151, 190, 215, 235-236,
        260, 270, 279, 287, 297, 304, 523
    immigrants 118, 128, 149, 232, 349,
        496
    Karāva 236
    middle class 304
    minority 5, 163, 270-284
    peasantry 246, 297
    ruling class 425
    status integration 243
    Veddas 128, 168, 230, 238
    women 5, 234, 239, 251-252, 273,
        295, 484
    youth 255, 263, 314, 426, 454
Social history of early Ceylon 87
Social institutions
    colonial period 116
Social issues 570, 584
Social policy
    British rule 118, 120, 128-129
*Social policy and missionary
    organizations* 128

Social problems 242-247, 248, 256
Social reform
    colonial policy 120
Social Science Research Centre 601
Social sciences
    bibliography 623
    periodicals 569-570, 587, 601-602, 613
Social services 246, 258-263, 269
Social stratification 229-239
    Kandyan period 113
    Sinhalese 236-237
    Tamil 229, 232, 235, 239
    women 239
Social structure 68
    contradictions 425
    ideal 214
    Kandyan kingdom 107, 113
    plantation workers 232
    matriclan 234
    Sinhalese 6, 110, 113
    Veddas 236
Social theory
    Kandyan Sinhalese 213
Social welfare 246, 257-269, 315
    colonial period 118
    policy 367
    population impact 171, 362
    women's access 239
Socialism 242, 311
Society 1-7, 28, 371
    artist's place in 514
    caste 128, 162, 229, 232, 234-236,
        241, 273, 279, 291
    classical 85, 91
    colonial period 2, 4, 14, 116, 491
    ethnography 206, 230-231, 233-234,
        238, 240
    Indian influence 9
    Kandyan 6, 113
    kingship 92, 419
    kinship 113, 168, 229-230, 234,
        240-241, 413
    marriage 113, 125, 229-230, 241,
        339, 413
    mediaeval 419
    monarchy 88, 92
    periodicals 570, 584, 607
    plural 273
    rulers 102-108, 475
    rural 260
    Sinhalese 1, 5, 79, 88, 205, 230, 234,
        236-237

189

190

Map of Sri Lanka

This map shows the more important towns and other features.

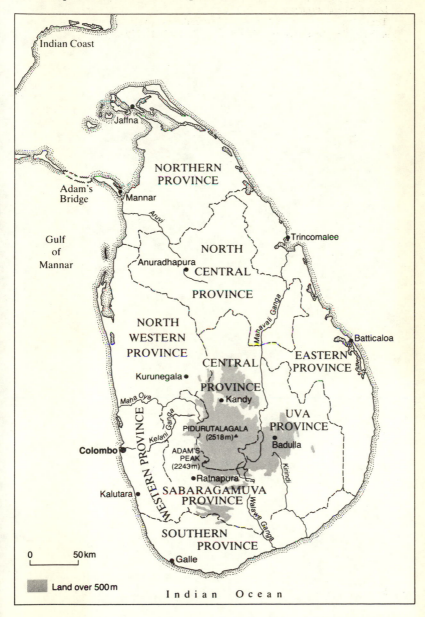

Indian Coast

Jaffna

NORTHERN
PROVINCE

Adam's
Bridge

Mannar

Aruvi

Gulf
of
Mannar

Trincomalee

NORTH
CENTRAL
PROVINCE

Anuradhapura

Mahaveli Ganga

NORTH
WESTERN
PROVINCE

Batticaloa

CENTRAL
PROVINCE

EASTERN
PROVINCE

Kurunegala

Maha Oya

Kelani Ganga

UVA
PROVINCE

Kandy

WESTERN PROVINCE

PIDURUTALAGALA
(2518m)▲

Colombo

ADAM'S
PEAK
(2243m)

Badulla

Kirindi

Ratnapura

SABARAGAMUVA
PROVINCE

Kalutara

Walawe Ganga

SOUTHERN
PROVINCE

0   50km

Galle

Land over 500 m

I n d i a n   O c e a n